MW01254869

The Pimp Game:
Secrets of Mind
Manipulation

by

Mickey Royal

Mickey Royal

Library of Congress Cataloging-in-Publication Data is available upon request.

Manufactured in the United States of America

Published by:
Sharif Publishing

Table of Contents

Dedication

"Ambiguity distracts the conscious mind. A little sleep, a little dream. All bodies – animals, plants, trees, water, even stones – are impregnated with this magic fluid, which might be propagated to a considerable distance."

Franz Mesmer
May 23, 1731- March 5, 1815

Entrance
by
Cheyanne Foxx
Adult Film Star

*He was somewhat shy, he caught my eye,
so I asked him to dance.
He took my hand, became my man, and put
me in a trance.
Every day was Christmas, every night was
New Year's Eve, I was the princess on his
arm.
He possessed a most dangerous allure,
deadly was his charm.
He put me on a pedestal, I was placed on
the top shelf.
He absorbed me into his world, that's when
I met Satan himself.
They were old friends, they went way back,
they knew each other well.
He offered me a ride, I never felt so alive,
so I rode with him to Hell...*

Chapter One
The Allure

The late-night Hollywood air possess an allure like no other. Standing on the corner of Hollywood and Vine one could take a deep breath inhaling the spirit that haunt these very streets. The ambience is electric to put it lightly. Hollywood is where dreams begin and stories end. Having played the game around the world only to be led right where I started. It's here I belong. There's no legal casino gambling here. No amusement parks. But lives are changed here every night.

Sunset boulevard, what an appropriate name for a street that comes to life at night. Vine Street, Fountain Ave, Sunset Blvd, Hollywood Blvd, La Brea Ave, La Cienega Blvd, Santa Monica Blvd, Highland Ave.

This is my jungle, the land off which I feed. Hollywood has fed many, but Hollywood also has a big appetite. How much can you eat before you get eaten? In the daytime, Hollywood looks like an amusement park for grownups. The Hollywood Wax Museum, Ripley's Believe it or Not, tour busses, The Chinese Mann Theatre, The Hollywood walk of Fame etc. For all appeared purposes Hollywood has a decent amount of family attractions. One might even catch a concert at the Hollywood Bowl or work out at Freddie Roach's Wildcard Boxing Gym.

But when the sunsets, these seemingly quiet streets come alive. Like the San Francisco 1849 Gold Rush, people from all over come to Hollywood to strike it rich or make it big. The risk is as high as the stakes. Never at a loss for lost souls. A city fueled by dreams and fantasies fulfilled hourly around the clock.

Hollywood, the land where time stops and resets at your disposal. You'll find the people on an entirely different frequency. The ones who are labeled 'off beat.' The one's who march to the beat of their own drum will find that song in rotation on the jukebox in Hollywood. The city where heaven and hell meet. It borders pain and pleasure running alongside ecstasy. This is where I've chosen to timelessly exist. You name the vice, I'll name the price.

On occasion it's been referred to as 'Hollyweird' by those on the outer rim in mockery. But to its inhabitants, it's revered for its ominous ambiance. A seemingly self-generated ever-present omnipotence flows from the lights, through the streets, through you, then back again. You become one with energy. In this city even the beat cops are writing and developing screenplays. A place where a conceptual idea is considered a tangible commodity. A place where you can be anything you want to be if you can get just one person to believe you.

When you're a career criminal, your record reads more like a resume. It serves as an invitation to few and a warning to most. The bigger your name, increases the likelihood of others looking to make a name from yours. Legends tend to take on a life of their own. True stories get passed from mouths to ears and so on and so forth. With each passing tale, I grew.

The problem with being 'The fastest gun in the West' comes from those who worship you to the point that they created the title for you. Then they begin to covet the position for themselves. They want the title without the pain (bullet holes and penitentiary time) that comes with it.

As the wheels of my Cadillac rotate counterclockwise, I'm compelled to recollect and re-evaluate my status from a distance to provide me with a panoramic view so I can properly assess the situation. Growing to legendary status from what comes naturally made my accomplishments look effortless. Being yourself is easy once you know who you are.

When one hears the word "Pimp," images of a sadistic Gorilla Pimp enters the minds of most. One having a cold cruel hand forcing young women to preform unspeakable sex acts for money. Women who by unfortunate circumstances find themselves unwilling pawns in the sex trade. Nothing could be further from the truth.

Forcing someone to do something they themselves wouldn't normally do, then taking the money from them and keeping it makes you a bully and an extortionist, not a pimp. Without guidelines and strict rules and regulations anyone can claim to be anything and attach what they do to a pre-existing definition thus altering the definition itself. This does an injustice to those who are in accordance with the rules and regulations. Those who over the years have sacrificed to shape, define and secure the very definitions themselves.

Those in violation will have to fit those oversized shoes they couldn't wait to wear. They've lied about the size of their feet in order to wear them. Wearing them is easy, walking and running in then will prove most difficult. Truth always comes to the surface eventually.

You can easily convince someone that you're someone else but never yourself. Empty unsubstantiated claims of being the fastest gun in the west will certainly put you in a position where you'll have to eventually draw. It takes time, energy, sacrifice and effort to become such a household name that your reputation precedes you. Time, energy, effort and sacrifice= dedication.

I've chosen my methods of operation as well as my activities. But I never chose my path. It chose me before I was old enough to make a conscious choice. I didn't begin this way. It was a gradual ascend or descend (depending on how you look at it) into what we call 'The Life'. Ironic, something referred to as 'The Life' that brings so much death.

It's a world where your first mistake may be your last. Where the lines of loyalty are drawn in the sand one minute and blown blurry like sand the next minute. Often referred to as 'The Game.'

So appropriate, since it's filled with players. In 'The Game' you're better equipped when you have an exit strategy before you conceive of entering. Some players have their team pre-assembled upon entering. Those players are unaware of the streets 'Free agent clause.' Any player may opt out of any agreement at any given time for any reason.

I expect the unexpected by having no expectations at all. But when drafting players on my team, they aren't ranked by good and bad. One could only do that in a game that never changes. Only then could someone take statistics based on results of performance. But in a game that shifts as much as 'The Game' does, one cannot judge his/her team players by any pre-set standard except their own.

You must set your own mark and enforce it. In this game, one could be a retired veteran before exiting puberty. These streets contain unlimited amounts of unbelievable stories yet to be told. The ones who lived 'The Life' usually don't live long enough to tell them. Being psychotic helps and is an attribute in this life.

When I was a young boy, I went to visit my grandparents in Memphis, Tennessee. They owned a farm on the land where their house sits. One day I was walking with my grandmother as she was feeding the chickens. While walking I asked her "What was the name of her cow?" She said "We don't name animals on a farm. If we name the cow, it makes it harder to swallow the T-bone steak later." Being psychotic makes it easier in this life to swallow the T-Bone steak later. And there will be steaks to swallow sooner or later.

"You don't know what you'll do till you're put under the pressure. Across 110th street is a hell of a tester" -Bobby Womack. The pressure and friction will produce a flawless diamond or dust. My Islamic upbringing then later converting to Shamanism, my martial arts training, my Zen way of life often comes in conflict with the world in which I existed. The perpetual paradox which is I. The fact that I'm able to find balance and make sense of it all only stands to affirm my psychosis.

We are who and what we do. No matter how you sneak up on a mirror it always looks you directly in the eyes. Resistance is futile. Acceptance is crucial. There are predators, prey and scavengers all on the prowl on any given night. Cloaked by a smile or the blinding shine of the sun as it reflects off overpriced jewelry.

Chapter 2
Seduced by The Darkside

When I was 13, I was a lookout for an
infamous drug dealer/kingpin. By age 14, I was his
chief enforcer. He barked and I bit. No questions
asked. I would report in every Saturday morning
around 9 a.m. It would already be soldiers and
lieutenants present. When he came down the stairs,
I would hear him say "Time to feed my greed." At
the time I was in the 8th grade and had no idea what
that meant. It wasn't until I got older, did I
understand what that meant.

He had no choice. He couldn't retire. He
couldn't take the money and walk away. He wasn't
in control, and he knew it. He was merely a vessel
of the Darkside IZM that coursed through his veins.
Operating under his tutelage acted as a crime
school. My tasks changed sometimes daily
depending on the situation.

I felt fortunate to be in such company and I
was going to do whatever it took to stay in such
company. "Time to feed my greed." In this life
going to prison can't bother you. If the possibility of

life in prison scares you, then you've chosen the
wrong life. Being incarcerated never bothered me.
In jail/prison I never go by Mickey Royal. I simply
go by Sharif. My birth/government last name. I
arranged for money to be deposited on my books.
I made weights out of plastic bags filled with water.
I began collecting fruit for Pruno (a homemade
wine), start my exercise routine and revert to my
Islamic studies, while diving deeper into my
Shamanistic practices.

Time, or the serving of comes with the
territory. There are no thorn-less roses. The game
will be good to you if you're good to the game.
Learn the rules thoroughly before you decide to
play. That mantra goes for any game. When you're
a career criminal, you must remain open to new or
different ideas and approach.
My mentor told me "You have one mouth but two
ears because listening is twice as important as
talking." You can't just be a fast learner. You must
be an immediate learner. You can find yourself out
of the game faster than you entered it.

At the age of 16, I was a religious fanatic.
With an Imam for a father and a former Black
Panther for a mother my political involvement was
predestined. I went to Marcus Garvey Elementary in
Los Angeles California. I was raised in the N.O.I
(Nation of Islam) and in high school I sold Bean
Pies on the corner of Crenshaw and Florence. I was
trained by and was under the direct order of Steve
Muhammad.

Steve Muhammad was a 10th degree Kenpo
master and Co-founder of the B.K.F (Black Karate

14

Federation). After my parent's divorce, there were many older men/mentors in my life clustered in a 4-year window filling the vacuum like void in the center of my soul.

There was Michael Conception (a former pimp and drug dealer who was one of the founding members of the Crips in 1971. He launched his record label Grand Jury Entertainment with the success of the "We're all in the Same Gang" project).

Imam Hamza (a former Crip turned Imam and was my spiritual guide throughout my high school journey). Steve Muhammad (my F.O.I. Captain and martial arts master. I learned as much outside the ring from him as I learned inside the ring).

Leslie Muwakal Mohammed (my 11th grade Afro-American history teacher at George Washington prep also a Vietnam veteran like Steve Muhammed. A musician and a master teacher. An African History historian and a trained psychologist). With him, I began my path of cultural anthropology and behavioral science.

Abdullah Ibrahim Binyahya (former prolific member of 'Malcom X' O.A.A.U Organization of African American Unity. He was one of the men who captured Talmadge Hagan, Malcolm's assassin. He taught me Arabic and started my path from the Nation of Islam to Sunni Muslim).

Donald Bakeer, Literature teacher. He was the first to recognize my talent for writhing and is mainly responsible for guiding me in that direction. Also, a former Vietnam veteran and F.O.I captain turned Sunni Muslim. He wrote the book South Central L.A Crips which was later turned into the movie 'South Central' starring Glenn Plummer directed by Oliver Stone).

I was in the company of these men everyday being taught. Leslie Mohammad, Donald Bakeer and Abdullah Binyahya all taught at Washing Prep High School. After school I was primarily with Mike Conception. Later that fizzed out and I was with Imam Hamza and Steve Muhammad. I learned all I could from them that they were willing to teach.

To me they represented a cluster. A mighty stone in which I crafted and sharpened my sword. Looking back, I can't help feeling nothing short of immense gratitude for having such masters in my life. Because of them, I'm never too busy to teach someone inquisitive enough to learn. Their doors for me were always open. But much like Anakin Skywalker I was seduced by the Darkside the Ism.

I had another mentor, Osiris Bey Kamal A.K.A. Siris. He was my introduction into the mystical powers of Shamanism. A wickedly wise man who would become my 'Lord Sidious' so to speak. A shaman and religious mystic master of the dark arts. He taught me how to manipulate karma as it relates to time.

All of my mentors lead me to a point to be exclusively trained by a criminal mystic. Black magic or 'Blacks magic' and 'Dark Arts' or 'Dark Artist' got its names from the people who practiced in the Ancient Ancestral Arts. From Central Africa deep in the valley of the fertile crescent, to the

Western coast of Africa and Eastern Europe and India to Haiti to New Orleans. From New Orleans to the cloaks of the religious underground and secret societies.

Let there be no misunderstanding, Osiris Kamal was a criminal. He tapped into a part of me I thought had died and he spoke directly to it. The sadistic element within myself buried deep within my subconscious. The more I learned, the deeper I got involved until I was in over my head. I was 18 and before I drowned, I learned how to tread then swim.

A year later I would meet Muhammad Salaam and Al-Ossrah (I wrote about in Along for The Ride). Another story for another time. Osiris Bey Kamal was murdered by someone he trusted. Apparently, he was at home entraining a friend because he had two wine glasses on the table and two plates. He went to open his wall safe and his guest shot him in the back 5 times and took the money from the safe while it was open. No one was ever arrested for the murder.

Osiris made his living pimping and doing 'Hits/security' for several high profiled drug dealers and entertainers. He was the perfect paradoxical paradigm. While working with him for a year as his sole apprentice I was able to gain the respect of everyone he dealt with. His contacts became my contacts and so on.

The Osiris I knew didn't sell drugs, but he told me he did back in Detroit in the late 60's early to mid-70's. Heroin to be exact. Osiris was born in New Orleans. I never knew his birthday, but he was a Capricorn. That's all I knew. I began my career in crime at age 13 as a lookout, making extra money to be spent on candy and Mrs. Pac Man. Later becoming muscle and so on, we had something in common to build on. He had a daughter in New York but no son.

I guess we filled each other's void. He was connected to the El Rukn's (Black Stone Rangers) out of Detroit, via Chicago. I often wonder what might have been had I never met him or made the choices I made. I often reflect whether or not I chose at all. No matter where you go, there you are. So be it.

My aunt found out I was a pimp and to say the least, she was disappointed. She made her opinion abundantly clear. She accused me of hating women. I told her nothing could be further from the truth. I told her I loved women and hold them in such esteem that I feel men should pay money just to be in their presence. The time women are in the presence of men should be compensated and appreciated.

Someone should put a price on that time and ensure that its IZM is not wasted or taken for granted. That someone is me. Women who've worked for or with me will tell you my dedication to the life was genuine. We are all living manifestations of the lessons we've learned along the way.

Like a soup or gumbo. A lot of different ingredients went into making, shaping, and building each and every one of us. Our parents, our teachers, our peers, and peer groups or activities, friends and relatives. That dangerous seductive allure I speak of is so powerful. It can touch you in ways that no other source can, in a place no other source can reach. The only limits that exist with your individual desires are within your own inhabitations.

I pride myself on being a messenger of sorts. A servant, if you will. My master is your subconscious. For it is you who created me. You who feed me. You who sustain and increase my power. The desires of man.

Most people will have to be asleep to experience their fantasies. You will experience your fantasies wide awake. You won't have to look far. Your aura will serve as a GPS tracker and those in relation to, will find you. As it relates. Deep with the human soul. Deeper within the human soul lies the human psyche. It speaks to the innermost resources, lodged deep within the subconscious, It speaks to the primal urges in the 'civilized' of human nature. Those urges will develop into a taste, then that taste will develop into a thirst and hunger for sustenance.

The most difficult as well as most rewarding is mastering self-control. To be in tune and in sync with your mind (conscious and subconscious) body and spirit. When you have total control of your pleasure, lusts, anger, emotions, actions, vanity, shame only then are you ready to start the journey of control over your destiny.

After that you will be ready to attempt to control the destiny of others as it relates to you. For every process there are stages. Always remember, history is being written in the present. The events of my life as it relates to me are inconsequential. I've stated on many occasions that I am the living manifestation of intense study. An embodiment of master teachers. To whom I will remain forever grateful. I took knowledges wisdom and understanding from them and returned to the streets via the allure.

One can't ever lie to one's self. Try it. Play tic tac toe against yourself. Each game will end in a cat's game (a tie). If you wish to learn about the moon you can ask an astronomer or Neil Armstrong. You will get an in-depth detailed description from one who's been there. I write it how I lived it. I've lived it as I knew it.

Have you ever known an alcoholic so long that they function in a permanent drunken stupor? They look and act as if they're drunk even though they might not have had a drink in months. The alcohol is so immersed in their blood that when they speak, their voice is permanently slurred. That's how immersed I am in the Ism. It used to come out in situations that didn't call for it. Anytime you saw me, I was in it.

But when you're truly a master you can cloak yourself as a Joe Schmo trick among tricks in order to achieve a greater reward to come. You'll be able to reveal yourself only by your command and in your chosen dosage.

Remember, when you first learned how to drive? You were so careful. Your hands were always at 10 and 2 on the steering wheel. Just one year later you were driving while eating a cheeseburger and changing the station on your radio all at once. Sugar Ray Leonard doesn't have to shadow box and work up his anger for an edge against an untrained street fighter. He's confident enough in his skills (time tested and proven) where his blood pressure wouldn't go above 120 over 80 while he's knocking the guy out.

I was once asked in an interview; Did I use violence against my mistresses (I detest the word Ho and all of the negative connotations that come with it) or wives? I answered her by saying the only time I used violence was against tricks who either got too rough or out of line with my wives. My violence was always used for their protection or in their defense.

That's why my record is full of assaults. Battery, and assault with a deadly weapon, attempted murder, reckless endangerment with a firearm. My women were my family and I went to jail and prison defending my family. Occupational hazard, it comes with the territory. This lifestyle or way of life isn't free. It will cost you things you otherwise can't afford to lose. Money will be the least of your losses.

After one bite of this forbidden fruit from the tree of knowledge (the Ism) you will never be the same. And you just may not like what your become. You'll be powerless to become your former self. Personally, I never had a former self.

I tasted the fruit in my formative years. My first orgasm was from an extreme act of violence, not an act of sex when I was 13. After that, I equated violence with orgasmic ecstasy.

Even being shot at 14 wasn't enough to deter me from the life. The more pain I inflicted as an enforcer, the more pain I needed to inflict to sustain a growing sadistic appetite.

My years as an F.O.I were some of the best years of my life. I had a dark secret and lead a double, oft times triple life. My mother use to say, "If you don't make a choice then a choice will be made for you." That statement became inexplicable prophecy. Things have a way of taking a natural course. Evolution if you will, without the assistance of man.

When anyone says the word 'molestation' ghastly images of sexual misconduct carried out upon a minor child enters the mind. In the Webster's dictionary I'm currently holding in my left hand it reads as follows; MOLEST- to interfere with or annoy. To accost sexually. To accost sexually was the second definition. The first definition was to interfere with or annoy. To interfere with says a lot.

A young child is much like a plant or tree. It is against the laws of nature and interferes with the process of development. Time dictates the agenda. When you disregard time and introduce an agenda before it's time, you'll forever warp the individual. They will never be able to regain balance or to once again be in sync.

I wrote a report in the 11th grade titled "I was molested, but not sexually." What makes child molestation or bestiality so unforgivable is the fact the child nor the beast had a choice. Therefore, it's technically rape. I was introduced to extreme acts of violence (permanent acts) when I was 13. I was still peeing in the bed. I had G.I. Joe action figures and a 22 revolver in my bottom bedroom drawer. I had just left the 6th grade and was entering the 7th. When the grown-ups put a child in a position where they a forced to grow up fast or partake in adult activities then that's molestation. The damaging effects are permanent.

I had to get older and look back at my trail of destruction to truly assess the damage. But it happened to me so early that it became a great part of who or what I became. I've never worked with a woman who wasn't raped or molested as a young girl. They all had been tampered with.

My particular demon was violence. I also developed an intense hatred for bullies. In high school, I felt it was my personal responsibility to protect the nerds and geeks. The weak or socially awkward, I gave and took many beatings for. I've always felt I was just a nerd who could fight. An intellectual if you will. At my age today, I have long outgrown self-evaluation questions or answers. "I've not the reason why. I've but to do or die" Alfred Lord Tennison.

The IZM can take on many forms as it consumes you. It can be words, philosophy, an ambiance, an atmosphere or lifestyle. The Ism can travel within its intoxicating allure. The next thing you know you'll be directing activities you once told yourself you'd never take part in. If desired, the metamorphosis can be quite enjoyable.

I accepted my destiny with open arms. From a meow, to a roar. As my mother use to put it

"In for a penny, in for a pound." I treated my mistresses with the utmost respect. I honored and revered them. I had developed and cultivated an individual relationship with each of them. That's why most of them today are my very close friends. No matter the occupation a woman is still a woman, with the same instincts and intuitions.

One woman I might have a father/daughter relationship. I might have a husband/wife, brother/sister and the older one's a nephew/auntie relationship. I properly referred to them as my mistresses of wives. They referred to each other as wife-in-laws. These were my wives. You didn't buy them from me, you rent them from me. Then you'd bring them back to me.

You'd buy their time and emotional obedience during that allotted time period. How can I abuse my family? I can't. But a pimp who constantly calls and refers to his wives as Ho's or Bitches will. Eventually abusive language proceeds physical abuse. Why would anyone of at least average intelligence bite the hand that feeds them?

Some pimps believe in breaking a ho down, thus lowering her self-esteem, so she won't ever think of leaving him. They feel destroying her self-esteem will keep her loyal. I always tried my best to raise my wives' self-esteem. For the same price, would you rather rent a Bentley or a Geo Prism

If a woman is to be in my personal space for any extended amount of time, then she'd better think highly of herself and self-worth. A pimp can only show you what they themselves have been shown. The title "The Hollywood King" I am sometimes referred to as, came about many years ago in my mid-twenties. It referenced more to my clientele than to me or individual skill.

I only take credit when credit is due. My clientele were quite a few Hollywood actors. I was known as the guy who could deliver any personal fantasy ordered. We would record the encounter on mini DV tape and copy ID's and model releases. When the encounter was over, I would personally burn the tape if front of the High Profiled client.

Why? This was so the encounter would be legal. The client sometimes chose to keep the tape and paperwork. No arrests could be made because no crime was committed. A legal sex tape was made. I never kept the footage either way. Blackmail is not a game.

My reputation is one of respect and reliability that didn't come easy. There is a code of honor in the life that includes hookers and bodyguards, and chuffers. We see but don't see and we never talk. We preserve the anonymity of our clients. Especially the high-profile ones (political, clergy and celebrities). The original copy is either destroyed in front of the client of so the client could choose to keep the tape to enjoy over and over again.

Whatever they ordered, I could and would deliver within the hour. From porn stars, Dominatrix, 18 yrs. old's who looked 13, themes like cheerleaders, girl scouts, nuns, MILF's, etc. some of the fantasizes would border on the extreme and bizarre to the outside ear. But I am impervious to shock. I swing fists and baseball bats, not gavels.

Before I knew it, I was receiving calls from wealthy couples to film them. Everyone wanted their own sex tape. One thing led to another and I ended up opening a porn production company (Cherry Hill Productions). I produced and directed 106 adult films. Gentlemen's video (Michael Esposito), Heatwave (Gabore), Cinderella Video (The Blackman's), Black market (J. Melendy). These were the main companies I produced and directed for but that's another story for another time.

There's no way of estimating where the allure will take you. It's definitely alive with a mind and heartbeat of its own. Tailor-made for the nocturnal, like myself. In recent years, this seemingly secret society of ours has become not so secret. This was not to my liking. The light began to shine in the mid to late 1990's. It's been all bad since then.

Vampire's burn in sunlight. And at best the nocturnal sleep during the light. The true vampires like myself run from the light (metaphorically speaking). Exposure can only bring heat (Law Enforcement). The only safe players were the retired ones. They could tell their stories in the past tense. Beyond the statute of limitations of course.

Being famous or infamous isn't good. For Jamie Foxx it's good, for Dr. Dre it's good, but for those who operate in the Underworld or the Shadow World, famous or infamy is the beginning of the end. Ask John Gotti did being in the public help or hurt him?

That was when I began going deeper into the

Shadow World through the back door of the Underworld, finally ending up starting a porn production company.

When I left, I took my crew (wives) with me. It wasn't cold turkey. It was a gradual transition. Most of my wives didn't want to leave but as a collective it was the right move to make at the time. Especially considering the rapidly changing atmosphere. The entire climate had begun to change overnight.

Sunlight is needed for growth. Sunlight into the Shadow World (The Pimp Game) only grew the interest of law enforcement, The I.R.S and young hoodlums. Young hoods, gangbangers who lacked the intelligence and finesse to conduct themselves properly as gentleman of leisure. When they entered the game, they brought an element of violence with them. Most of them were unaware that they were already under the surveillance of police for their violent and narcotic activities.

The Pimp Game has always been loose, but tight at the same time. This is a game of skill, finesse, and intelligence. It's a gentlemen's game, like chess. From out of nowhere, entered not so gentlemanly checker players. All of a sudden, I found myself in shootouts with gangsta's (not gangsters). If I didn't have the background that I have, I wouldn't have won those altercations.

It took me back to my teen years. When something is imbedded in you, you can always bring it out when the situation calls for it. But some of my fellow 'Gentlemen' were not so fortunate. The young gangsta's began playing chess with checker's rules. They were kidnapping ladies right in broad daylight. Selling them like pieces of property. Beating and torture became common practices. They began human trafficking, forced and held captive. Several ladies were murdered.

The real players like myself put our backs to the wall and sat back and watched the gangsta's vs. the Feds title match... The Feds won. It got ugly. The Feds created a human trafficking task force. They used weapons like the Rico Act, the Mann Act, and pre-existing laws against 'White Slavery'. But when the Feds dropped the hammer, it came down upon gangsta's and gentleman the same.

The Feds made no distinction between the two. Pimps or Gentlemen of Leisure who were accustomed to going to Federal Prison for tax evasion for 1 to 3 years or a pandering change were now being handed down 25 to life sentences. Some causes even higher.

Before the gangsta's entered the game, policemen and firemen were some of my best clients. I used to arrange all of their bachelor parties etc. They knew me, my wives and we all conducted ourselves with mutual respect.

Before all of the movies and documentaries, we operated with impunity. We provided a community service in a way. That's what ignited the flame inside of me to pick up my pencil again and set the record straight. In high school and Jr. high school, I wrote primarily songs and screenplays during my leisure time. I picked the pencil up again many years later and wrote The Pimp Game: Instructional Guide (at age of 26).

I wrote it in response to what I was witnessing. I wrote "The Pimp Game Instructional Guide while I was still living 'Along for the Ride.' Then I wrote "Along for the Ride." Those two books reunited me with my first love... writing. Before the crimes, before the mentors, before the women, there was me, my notebook and my pencil. I had come full circle.

In the movie 'The Godfather part 1, Don Vito Corleone is speaking to his Consigliere (councilor) Tom (Robert Duvall). Tom is telling him about a narcotics dealer named simply "The Turk." The first thing Don Vito asked Tom was "What about his prison record?" Tom tells Don Vito that The Turk has done time in Turkey and Sicily.

If you're a Career Criminal and you have a clean record, then you're one of the three;

1. A liar
2. A snitch
3. A cop

The penitentiary comes with the life. That you can count on. Whenever I go on vacation (prison) I have my Quran, dictionary, push-ups, pencils and paper. I go by my legal last name "Sharif." The Pimp Game isn't a hustle, it's a lifestyle, a chosen lifestyle for Hedonistic entrepreneurs. Currently it's a shell of its former self. A once upon a time story for days past. Some of the true players still operate deep within the shadows.

It's come full circle. But on windy

Hollywood nights like this, I love to go to the roof and just sit by the swimming pool and write. Sometimes I prefer to walk the Blvd amongst the people and absorb the collective 'Chi.' I'd make my way to Pink's hotdog stand on La Brea Ave. My crew (family of wives) the Royal Family, were able to weather the storm and evolve when it became critical to our survival.

At the base of my business was a sincere sense of family. At the end of the day, that's all that mattered. Over the years, my lifestyle hasn't changed. Only my activities have. I still enjoy handwriting my books in pencil. Keyboards lack passion and passion is an element I'm loaded with.

The game was good to me because I was good to it. In 2015 I was in LA county jail on the same floor as Suge Knight. He was in Orange (High Profile) I was in Browns (Bi-Polar and Diabetic). He was down the hall from me on the 8000 floor.

I was convicted and sentenced to 5 years for Attempted Murder but pled guilty to Assault with a Deadly Weapon for less time. In 2013, I was in LA county jail. Chris Brown was there although I never say him. I was in 4300 Able row cell 10. 2014, I was in dorm 8030 the 8120. Also, in 2014 I was in 2300 able row. 2015 I was in Wasco State prison. 2016 I was in Chino (C.I.M) State prison. 2014 was another assault case. 2011, I was convicted in Van Nuys on a gun charge.

I could go on and on. Incarceration never bothered me. It served no purpose. It didn't motivate nor discourage my actions. I am who and what am. My resume' is full. My goal is to never return. But if I must, I must. Through the anonymity of the internet, people can easily pretend to be something they're not. Some of these masqueraders live totally lied lives behind a computer. They feel they can say and do what they want without retribution or accountability. They have 'Dot com coverage' just like some men have to get drunk to express themselves verbally or physically. We call them "Beer Muscles."

The Pimp Game; Secrets of Mind Manipulation

Chapter 3
Pathway to Immortality

In ancient folklore, there exist an ongoing feud. A rivalry between the Likens and the Ever-living (Vampires). These tales based in truth have survived the ages. Although unseen by the untrained eye, the two forces are able to identify one another. Both possess a dangerous allure felt instantly in their presence. Later the Likens adopted a more suitable name. One made impossible not to know who or what they are: Werewolves.

The Ever-living also adopted a more suitable name. One that possessed an instant mystique: Vampires. Both Werewolves and Vampires operate by night. Lurking in the shadows. Both looking for victims to bite. A bite from either can kill you or transform you into one of them, thus increasing their individual power, and power of the collective. The two opposing factions are both subservient to the power of the moon and its lunar calendar.

33

Although very similar, there are distinctive differences. These differences make it impossible for the two to work together for an extended period. Only uniting briefly to vex a common enemy. Neither will ever trust the other.

The distinct differences between them are: Werewolves are pack hunters and Vampires operate alone with one ghoul. The Ghoul acks like as henchman and guards the coffin while the Vampire sleeps in the day. Werewolves take on a more savage approach. Whereas vampires take on a more sinister approach.

A vampire may have 3 to 5 wives he calls "Brides." Werewolves travel in packs of 20 or more. Their strengths are in their numbers. This rivalry of characteristics has its roots in the animal kingdom. The Lions (Vampires) and the Hyena (Werewolves). One is a predator and the other a scavenger. The Hyena's are known to travel in packs up to 20. They lack size a strength individually but, in a pack, they are a dominant and dangerous force.

Lions travel in prides. They consist of one to two males and 4 to 7 females. The females do all of the hunting and will bring the food to the male so he can eat first. The males do all of the fighting, the females will not assist him. If the male lion loses to another male lion, the females of the looser now belong to the winner.

In the natural order of the status quo; Its "predators hunt and kill the food and the scavengers wait and eat what they leave behind." But sometimes the hyenas don't feel they should wait. Why should 30 wait on 7? The conflict continues.

In humans who co-exist in an almost paralleled universe, this rivalry continues today. You have those of the Underworld against those of the Shadow world competing for control of the night. The same battle of characteristics continues between pimps (vampires) and gangsters (liken/pack hunters).

Gangsters think pimps are weak. Pimps think gangsters are stupid. Both take life and death chances. A clash of lifestyles and idealisms. One sells a product the other provides a service, both have more in common then they care to admit. There lies an undertone of disdain for one another covered by a thick coating of mutual respect.

The one advantage that the Ever-living (vampires) have over the Liken (Werewolves) is as true in folklore as it is on the streets; Vampires can change form from a vampire (the undead) to a bat and even a wolf. He is able to cloak himself (go undercover) as a werewolf but only temporally. It's like flexing a muscle.

The werewolf can only take on two forms: One as a human and the other a werewolf. He can't cloak himself as anything other than what he is: Half man, half wolf but the werewolf can hunt by day or night his human side insures this.

You may find a vampire traveling in twos. Him and his Zombie (Igor or ghoul) who is cultishly loyal, because he is trapped in the allure of the vampire the same as his brides. I make the parallel. A pimp can appear as a gangster. A gangster can't appear as a pimp.

A lot of pimps started out as young gangsta's. Very few, if any gangsta's started off as pimps. I've known pimps who became envious of the seemingly effortless large sums of money gangsters were making selling drugs. Especially in the 1980's.

The pimps I knew who got into that unfamiliar game were largely unsuccessful. They tried to bring civilization to a savage environment and quickly became prey. The gangsters met with the same fate while in The Pimp Game. They brought savagery to a gentlemen's game and were everything but gentle. Their methods forced the heavy hand of law enforcement and ushered in new laws and legislation. The only thing the gangsters did was created a category for themselves 'Human Traffickers.'

That category became their coffin. They dug their own grave and the Feds buried them 25 years deep. Solo gangsters/hustlers have about as much success as pimp gangs. You can't run PC software on a MAC. You can't run MAC software on a PC. The two machines are not compatible. Gangstering is a team sport. Pimping is a solo sport. In pimping, the closest you get to a team is your stable. And that's a family at best. In gangstering the closest you get to a solo operation is that of a Kingpin and even he must share, eventually.

Both dabble safely in each other's realm. The safest way to dabble is to keep in mind that this is <u>not</u> your house. You are only a guest. If you act as a respectful visitor, then your presence will be welcomed.

When both are on point, they can co-exist as allies. This is feasible but usually unlikely. Both are powerful in their own rights. With great power, comes great responsibility. To the righteous at heart great power will make him more responsible. But to those who only look inward. This great power can destroy the powerful who possess it.

The inward develop conceit, arrogance, megalomania, sac-religiousness, self-righteousness and the overwhelming feeling of an exaggerated sense of one's own self value. That would be the type of self-serving egomaniac who will be currently involved in illegal business and agree to go on a documentary of cable T.V. and in theaters and not only admit to the crimes. But brag about them in detail.

An individual that foolish doesn't deserve to be in the game. Those individuals had the nerve to look surprised when they got arrested. Now that's an egomaniac. Another big distinction between the life of a gangster and the lifestyle of a pimp is that the gangster life doesn't always come home. A gangster or racketeer is allowed to have a wife and children.

Most of the time his family has no knowledge that he's involved in criminal activities. He can clock in and clock out at the end of his workday. He may keep odd hours, but he leaves the rackets in the street. The pimp is not allowed to have an outside life. He's not allowed to have wives in the game and a separate square wife at home. His wives are usually in the home with him. He's at work when his wives are at work.

37

He's at work when his wives are asleep. The wives work the tricks, the pimp works the wives. He has to be in their heads without losing his. The only way a pimp can have a square life is to leave the game entirely, then go get married. But most pimps have been in the game so long that they're clueless of how to conduct themselves in a "Normal Relationship."

A pimp sees himself as married to his wives. The wives see themselves as married to the pimp. Even if and when their activities may change over the years and the pimp grows and develops, the wives grow and develop with him.

I once owned a soul food restaurant. My bodyguard was one of my cooks along with my bottom women. The three waitresses were also from the stable. My star worked the counter where we kept pastries and pies and I worked the register. My star would work the register only during my bank runs.

We once owned an adult video store. That business catered to our very nature. My point being whatever I did or wherever I went, I took my wives with me along for the ride. I used to envy the gangsters who seemed to be able to have their cake and eat it too. They were able to have a square home life and a street life. Those dual options aren't available to pimps unfortunately.

I personally had an advantage over most pimps. Most pimps started out as hustlers first. They began pimping around age 20. I started out a gangster/hustler at the age of 13. I went from gangster to Hustler/Muscle.

By the age of 15 it was 1987 and the crack wars of L.A. were in full swing. By the time I started pimping in my early 20's, I was already a veteran career criminal. The Pimp Game suited my new lifestyle just fine.

Since the age of 14, I had been used to having sex with grown women. Grown women who want crack cocaine will screw a 14-year-old crack dealer in a heartbeat. My bi-polar disorder imbalanced brain was tailor made to carry out my sociopathic duties. It never bothered me. I saw myself as a soldier. There were always beautiful women around. They enjoyed just being in our presence.

As I grew older and made a transition into pimping my entourage grew smaller. The unhappiest years of my life were the 5 years I squared up and became a regular Joe Schmo. At the end of the day you've got to be yourself. What choice do you have?

I learned the pimp game from Osiris. He was the final tuner of my piano and I played beautiful songs metaphorically speaking. Osiris was rumored to be a member of a secret underground crew of Islamic Pimps called the 'Red Devils'. They were known to conjugate around the Vermont and Century area.

The streets are compiled of rumors, legends and tales. He never spoke on the and I never asked him about them. I do know he grew up in and was a member of the Moorish Science Temple. By the time I met him he was heavy in Zen Meditation. He put the finishing touch in what would later become

Mickey Royal. I chose my mentors carefully based on individual qualities they possessed that I wanted to obtain. I chose mentors who primarily had daughters or no sons at all. This were by design.

I had to be their primary interest. Not merely a student, but an apprentice. I saw my 7 mentors (Sijo Steve Muhammad, Michael Conception, Imam Hamza, Leslie Muwakal Mohammed, Donald Bakeer, Abdullah Binyahya, and Osiris Bey Kamal) nothing short of Gods in flesh. I am the living manifestation of excellent teachers and mentors. But it was Osiris who brought me completely over to the Darkside.

Most people who knew me, my parents and my upbringing predicted that would be a political activist, or a teacher. My mother thought I had the calling to be an Imam (Islamic Minister). She didn't know at the time that call was already a busy signal. My mother has always loved me but never understood me. I pray nightly for her forgiveness... and my own. My father stopped speaking to me when he found out I was in the adult film business. I shielded my parents and relatives away from my life/lifestyle as best I could. My father didn't know that the 106 adult films I produced and directed were the least wicked of my endeavors.

I've never been a pillow talker and I always kept my business on a need to know basis. I want my tombstone to simply read "Mikail Sharif A.K.A. Micky Royal "Writer." If there was one word to describe Mickey Royal, it would be "Writer". That's the one word I use to describe myself. Other than the word 'Writer' I don't label or self-evaluate.

I didn't give myself the name 'Mickey Royal.' A woman named 'Gorgeous' did. Beware the man (in this Game) who <u>needs</u> attention. Why? Because he'll get it. But not from the sources of his intent. Let others toot your horn. They eventually will, whether you want them to or not. In this life if your name is on too many tongues rest assured your file is on somebodies' desk.

I can honestly say if I never met Donald Bakeer, I wouldn't be writing books today. To this day, I still consort Muwakal. A wise and talented man who has successfully navigated me through some of life's biggest challenges. I honor and keep my word, even if it costs me. I've never burned a bridge in my life and I never will.

A good reputation can take a lifetime to build and only one moment to destroy. I protect my reputation and stand by it. At this point my reputation precedes me. "A man who doesn't have his word is a cockroach"-Tony Montana.

I've only accepted top notch women into my family. Looks were important but not most important, attitude and manners were. The way I saw it, I was introducing a foreign element into an established unit. It had to be conducive to my well-oiled machine. My family didn't need fresh fish. To get with me on the level I was on, you had to have something special about you. Something exceptional that no one but you could offer.

I've turned down and turned away more than I excepted. They had to mesh well with me but especially my wives. She had to be smart and she had to be a quick and eager learner. The first sign of dissension no matter how small and she's gone. I moved at a pace where I had no time, patience or room for such behavior.

Most of my mentors were good hearted, god-fearing, law-abiding men I know on one hand I let them down with my chosen path, but I needed to have what they possessed and the only way to get it was an apprenticeship. Much later in life, I was taken under the wing of Michael Esposito C.E.O. of Gentlemen's Video in Chatsworth California. He was the son for reputed mobster Salvador Esposito. I learned a lot from this 'Man of Respect.' We developed a true friendship. I've considered taking on an apprentice of my own. To master the IZM.

Chapter 4
Nouns; Persons, Places and Things

Gorilla Pimp - Some people spell it Guerilla (as in an organized militia) pimp. The proper spelling is Gorilla (as in big dumb ape). Most people hear the word "pimp" and the behavior and tactics of a Gorilla pimp comes to mind. Why? Because Gorilla pimps are the largest group of pimps.

Over half of the pimps I've ever met or dealt with were Gorilla pimps. The Gorilla pimp isn't the brightest bulb on the tree. He's all brawn, very little brains. He knows his hoes are smarter than him, so he is never too far away from them. He controls by force using violence and fear tactics to enforce submission.

Any sign of abnormality and the Gorilla Pimp will use anything at his disposal as a weapon (wire hanger being his favorite). He lacks skill, finesses and understanding. Another weapon in his arsenal is humiliation. Not just to break her, but as a common practice. He is in constant fear of being outsmarted or out witted by his ho's, so he is constantly beating them down in attempts to crush their spirit.

He is a covert sadist, and an overt misogynist. He takes delight in calling her a 'Bitch.' He doesn't possess the ability to evolve. He doesn't treat his women like family. They're his subjects and he's their subjugator. The Gorilla Pimp is the pimp who is most likely to use underaged girls. His women choose him because they have absolutely nowhere to go. His women are the homeless, the runaways, the women who can no longer support their drug addiction, women who've been recently evicted. Those are his prey.

You'll find him on weeknights circling the Greyhound bus station, scouting for desperate women. The Gorilla Pimp's women are the ones most likely to turn on him and deliver him to law enforcement.

The C.E.O Pimp – C.E.O (Chief Executive Officer) Pimp runs his stable like a fortune 500 company. He uses logic and mathematics to make his decisions. Sometimes referred to as a 'No Nonsense Pimp.' He pimps accordingly and enforces strict rules and regulations. He is always looking to expand. He takes pride in the financial output of his ho's.

He's the most selective of pimps. Quality not quantity is his aim. Unlike the Gorilla pimp, you won't see him in flashy clothes and jewelry. He's not a star, he's a star maker. He's empty, cold and calculating. His power lies deep within his anonymity. Only a select few will know his name. Everything is on a need to know basis.

He may have ties to organized crime. He will appear more Mafia-ish than Pimp-ish. You will find him shuffling up the crowd (his ho's). Example: The C.E.O Pimp will have as much activity for his ho's as possible.

They won't just get on the track and stay there all day and night. He prefers opening brothels and unionized styled, escorts services. His ho's activities may include the track, the strip club, private in call escorting, outcall escorting, porn productions movies, photo shoots, after hours, bachelor parties, webcam and website work.

Comparable to Charlie Angels (T.V show), the itinerary can change daily. The C.E.O Pimp is only visible when he has to be. He usually travels in pairs, himself and a bodyguard, and or driver. He speaks only when spoken to and may dabble in outside interests such as narcotics or legitimate enterprises.

He treats his ho's with dignity and respect without familiarity. He is the pimp most likely to profit share. His pimp style comes from the world of legitimate business. Unlike the Gorilla Pimp who takes 100% of his ho's earnings. The C.E.O. Pimp may take only 35% to 50% and he covers expenses out of his end. The Gorilla Pimp will have 3 hos' giving him 100% while the C.E.O pimp may have 12 Ho's giving him 35%.

45

Gorilla Pimps adds, the C.E.O Pimps multiplies.

Romeo Pimp – The Romeo Pimp is more
commonly known as a Chili pimp or Boyfriend
pimp. 'Boyfriend Pimp' being the more accurate of
the descriptions because he is just that. By
definition, he is a pimp, technically. Although those
in the game would question his validity.

He convinces his girlfriend to become a ho
"temporarily." He says is reason is for them to get
the two for them out of a particular financial jam.
He only as one ho. She is his girlfriend or baby
mama. She is one woman feeding two or more
mouths, so they never seem to make any progress.
If he had two ho's it's because one is his girlfriend
and the other is either his girlfriend's friend or
girlfriend (romantically speaking).

Look for the two or three of them to be
living in a motel paying by the night for long term
stay. Romeo Pimp fancies himself as a manager. He
will often become jealous of his ho's A.K.A his
girlfriend's tricks and is subject to lash out violently
at the paying customer. If doing well (and that's a
big if), you will find this dumbfounded duo working
the casino floor in Vegas. He has no idea what it
takes to be a real pimp, but he wants to do
desperately.

This particular pimp got his game from
movies, T.V. and rap lyrics. His style indicates that
he had no mentor and he started in the game far too
late. His ho/girlfriend has no respect for him
because she works, and he perpetrates. He's living a
fantasy at her expense.

She may actually enjoy Hoing but not for him. He's more like the little brother or child in her eyes that she feels she must protect and support. Her true love for him has her trapped in a downward spiral.

<u>Pimpster</u> – The Pimpster is a new character and recent player in the game. He deserves mention and recognition because he is rapidly becoming a major influence and percentage wise, he's just under Gorilla pimps. Gorilla Pimps are primarily in the Midwest and deep south. Whereas the Pimpster is in major metropolitan cities.

If you notice, his name is a Hybrid. He's half pimp and half gangster. By definition and activity, he is a pimp, but his swag and style are that of a gangster. He was raised during the rap music era. He will be under the age of 30. He has a background in various other crimes. He runs his stable of ho's like a street gang applying street gang tactics.

His hos are young also. They steal as much as they date (sleep with a client). You won't find him driving a Cadillac, he will be in an expensive Japanese (Lexus) for German (Mercedes) car. Pimpster's are known to run in packs, forming actual 'pimp gangs' which totally goes against traditional practices. His ho's most likely started out as members of the same street gang as the Pimpster. Therefore, when he added pimp to his resume the females in the gang added ho to there's without question.

"The gang (set) needs you to do this." His

ho's will most likely engage in small narcotic sales and theft while on the track. Pimpsters are always on the lookout for set ups. Example: If his Ho's happens to have a rich trick, rest assure the Pimpster and members of his gang may interrupt that session wearing ski masks.

Human Traffickers – Human traffickers are not Pimps. They're kidnappers and slave traders. I included them in this segment for two reasons: 1). The government has included pimps into the human trafficking category. 2. I want people in the Game/Life to beware of these roving groups of sexual predators and kidnappers. Keep your eyes and ears open. Modern day slavery is the politest way of describing this heinous criminal practice. The Human Traffickers that I've come in contact and conflict with were from other countries. Egyptians, Armenians, Mexicans, Russians, Asians (primarily Chinese), and New York Jamaicans.

The Egyptians pay 30,000 per person. The women have no idea what is about to take place. She will be drugged and wake up overseas. The Armenians grab un-suspecting American women and hook them on Heroin. They end up in an abandoned apartment building or cellar in little Armenia in Los Angeles. They are watched 24 hours a day, 7 days a week. The Armenians charge the tricks less than 100 dollars while all profit is kept by Armenian gangsters.

The Mexicans take full advantage of the fact that Mexico borders the United States. They work from both angles. Women in Mexico have made deals with Coyotes to get then across the border. The women agree to work in these "Houses" for an undisclosed amount of time. The Mexican American gangs take Mexican American women and girls deep into Mexico to be sold as sex slaves.
The Russian Mafia covers the gamut of the sex trade. From kidnapping American women and selling them overseas, to setting up "houses" (underground brothels), to smuggling "mail order" non-English speaking Russian girls and women as sex slaves to wealthy American men (disguised as domestics, maids and nanny's).
The Chinese have the ports of the U.S under control. Asian women (Philippian, Thailand, China) are sold and some are set up in brothels with "massage parlor" fronts which advertise in newspapers promising "Happy Endings".
The Jamaicans posse's take women in American and set up underground sex dens in NY basements. The women stay under the perpetual threat of violence visited upon their families.

Candyman – A Candyman is the younger version of a Sugar daddy. A Candyman uses his candy (money) as power to women in dire straits. He appears as a savior and showers her and her children with gifts and attention, at first. He may "give" her a car (in his name) and necessities at crucial moments. His game is to get her feet firmly on the rug before he snatches it or not, but has the power to.

After she gets use to him to the point where his contributions are absolutely necessary for her continued survival is when he makes his move. He will start slow and begin his plan gradually. It may start with something as simple as a threesome with her best friend. He will begin to push the envelope ever so slightly. He's testing the waters to see how far he can go and hot much she will take.

After she has developed a taste of the good life he can provide, she is compelled to obey his every command from walking the track to delivering a "package." Her desires and fear of returning to her former life locks her in.

She knows a "no" answer for any of his requests, no matter how bizarre, will result in her immediate expulsion from his atmosphere that she now breaths. She is his slave.

Women in her world (aunts, mother, daughter, niece, cousins, sisters, best friends) will see her shining via his light and grow envious of her, thus drawing them closer to his flame. Candyman will transform his woman into his bottom women and the women in her world will become his stable.

Because her circle of friends won't change (only their activities will), it will all seem normal to her as well as her idea. The other ladies will consciously and unconsciously compete for the top spot. Like crabs in a barrel each one will keep the next one in line.

Sugar Daddy – Candymen get old and turn into Sugardaddys. Sugardaddys are usually upwards in age 55+. He knows every aspect of the game. In his younger days he may have been a Pimp, Mack, Candyman or even a Hustler. He wasn't a trick when he was younger, but he decided to take on a trick's persona in order to enjoy some of the spoil's tricks get to freely partake in.

Well, not free of course. The Sugardaddy is mainly having a good time. He is not to be underestimated. Sugardaddy's know the IZM. He has purposely put himself in the position of a trick. He also has the power to travel through the IZM. Whatever he used to be, he can easily go back to being in a flash. He's not your ordinary trick.

He will usual have only one woman he is showering with gifts. She refers to him as her "friend." The entire family may know him as her Sugardaddy. He doesn't get to know the family, only to know of them. She is in the position of a Ho or a mistress with only client. She may also have a full-time boyfriend. This is feasible because the Sugardaddy visits sporadically, but never without calling.

His visits take precedence over anyone and anything even if she is with her boyfriend. She may create a reason to send him away on an errand. The boyfriend may or may not know of him. Either way it doesn't matter.

Sugardaddy's are the preferred clients of Ho's who have Romeo pimps. Because Romeo is so unskilled in the game, a Sugardaddy represents consistent income.

Romeo gets to live a lie to himself as a 'real pimp' while he's actually trying to figure the game out.

Pimping P.I. - P.I. stands for 'Pimping International.' This is title added as a suffix to an existing pimp's name. Example: I would introduce myself or be introduce as "Mickey Royal P.I." or I would say the entire phrase "Mickey Royal Pimping International." This title or tag must be earned and verified.

It's more of an extra added bonus than a rule of thumb. But the tag is mis-labeled. The word 'International' implies that the pimp has pimped outside of the United States. In the game you get the tag if you've consistently pimped in other states. There is a distinct difference between P.I. and 'Cross-Country' pimping.

To pimp P.I. you have to have set up shop in other cities/states and consistently go back and forth collecting in those cities and states. Example: If you're based out of Los Angeles and you have a thriving stable, and you take 2 – 3 Hos with you to Houston TX. Build up a stable there. When you get back to Los Angeles and your Bottom Woman hands you an envelope, you're pimping P.I. But the stables you left in other cities are still producing cash and you stop through one week per month to all of them that's pimping P.I. That's the way I was taught.

Cross Country Pimping – The meaning of this is closer to its label. Example: You take some of your Ho's on the road. You hit hot spots and tracks along the way. You may have specific events like Spring Break, the N.B.A. Allstar game after party, Championship Boxing after parties, Camp Pendleton (service men's payday), Grammy Awards after parties etc. Afterwards you and your Ho's return to your city of origin. That would be considered Cross Country pimping. Before going cross country, a pimp must do his homework thoroughly.

Con Man – The term Con man is short for 'Confidence Man.' We're mostly familiar to what a Con man is. We have confidence pimps out there. He is a complete waste of a real Ho's time. He has the flashy car and clothes that his mother or square job bought hm. He's no more than a lying thief. He puts on a big presentation to captivate a Ho. He has no IZM whatsoever. He's all about "Cop and Blow," get all you can and then you go.

I remember when the big hustle for Confidence pimps were 'Fly-by-Night' modeling agencies. They would spend most of their money on an excellent location and business cards. He advertises in the publications where the desperate and the eager go looking for opportunity. The ladies answer the modeling ads. The Con Man takes photos of her. He sends her to a few auditions. Then he tells her she needs new pictures. He hires a photographer and she pays him 1,000 dollars for pictures that land her about two gigs worth 4 hundred dollars each.

Unbeknown to the young ladies that it's all a con. He may have 50 – 100 women he's running this game on. The gigs are his partners, co-conspirators in the criminal set up. That's just one for starters. If it sounds 'too good to be true,' it probably is. Legit modeling agencies don't ask for money. If your manager or agent, asks you or require you to make as much as a $.05 deposit, then it's a con.

Pusher Pimp – a Pusher Pimp or Drug Pimp is sinisterly sadistic. His game about 100% control. He deals with Ho's who are either addicted to drugs or Ho's he can get hooked on drugs. Their addiction to the drug (supplied by him) leads them to a life of prostitution. A pusher pimp makes sure she has no other connect (drug contact person) so she can ONLY get the drug from him. He becomes the sole provider.

Example: He may give his crack-cocaine addicted Ho a 20-dollar rock to get her started. She makes 300 dollars and he gives her another rock. It's a reward and punishment system with instant gratification. The Pusher Pimp knows he can't leave his crack, meth or heroin addicted Ho unattended because her addiction will have her leaving her post and taking the money to go and get high. The Pusher Pimp watches her 24 - -7 and must collect after every single date.

Player (Hustler) Pimp – Those who are familiar with my previous works, know I don't like to use the word 'Player' to describe anyone specific. I feel everyone in the Game is a player. Except the trick. The trick is not a player, but he is a participant.

But for informational and explanatory purposes I will use the term 'player.' I personally prefer to call them Hustler Pimps.

The Player/Hustler Pimp has deeper IZM than people expect him to have. His power lies in his patience and the way he carries himself. The Player is suave, sophisticated, well read, and nothing ever seems to bother him. A player has his hands in more than one cookie jar. He usually has two Ho's tops. They keep him together and he keeps them moving forward.

Since he doesn't have a stable, his two Ho's are saturated in the IZM and share his power as equal players. Everything is split evenly. He doesn't have the time nor desire to invest fully in The Pimp Game. Look for the Player to have skills in larceny, narcotics, murder for hire, gambling etc.

The Player Pimp isn't stationary. He moves and shakes. His Ho's never work the track. They do high priced In-calls, for select clientele. The Player Pimp will remind you more of Clark Gable or James Bond, than a pimp. He's definitely a renaissance man.

The Madam – The Madam is a pimp. She is not to be confused with the Bottom Woman. The Madam is a female pimp who usually has a large stable. Much like the C.E.O. Pimp, she unionizes and profit shares. She multiplies while most pimps add.

The Madam usually takes 50%. Out of her 50% she covers all expenses. Unlike the C.E.O. pimp and the Corporate Charlie's Angels style, The Madam's style remains homely. Her "Girls" as she refers to them are like her daughters. She is usually at least 20 years older than her "girls." She is an ex Ho who mastered the IZM.

Her stable can be from 5 – 20+. She is an attractive woman (for her age) who dresses in lingerie' all day. She may have Ho's on the track but not usually. A Madam's stable is 95% 'In-call' and 5% cross country events. The In-call insures her and her stable's safety.

She always has live-in security. He is not a pimp, just paid muscle. She will enforce discipline when necessary, without hesitation. She is as ruthless as she is cunning. She usually has a good working relationship with police. Her style is discrete and above reproach.

She's in the Game for the long haul. Her Ho's feel the warmth from her 'Foster-Home' style. The madam may have her 'girls' working out of a massage parlor if her home isn't large enough. She needs a large home to accommodate so many girls. Look for her to have a huge home in a rural area. Or a massage parlor in the city.

Playboy = a fun-loving trick who refuses to reject a good time and has the wallet to support his insatiable appetite.

A Gentleman of Leisure = The correct term for a pimp. The word 'Pimp' is something pimps are called by the squares. But we refer to ourselves as Gentlemen of Leisure.

After Hours = An underground speakeasy. An illegal club which operates without permits. Hookers, stripping, gambling, narcotics and alcohol are readily available between the hours of 2:am to 6: am.

Stuffing = Is when a Ho is skimming profits. Example: She made 800 dollars but turned in 500 to her pimp. She 'stuffed' 300 dollars.

Date = When a Ho has sex with a client for money it's called 'A Date.' Date' has replaced that term 'turn a trick.' A date is milder and more suitable for overheard conversations.

G.F.E. = 'Girl Friend Experience' describes the type of service a Trick would receive. A GFE is more personable and last longer and cost more than an ordinary 'Date.'

Greek = A term that simply means 'anal sex.'

Roses = Is slang for dollars.

The Shadow World = It's ran paralleled to the Underworld but of a sexual nature. Pimps, Mack's, Ho's, Human Traffickers, Swingers, Orgies, Porn, Prostitution, After Hours, Bordello's all exist in The Shadow World.

Bottom Women, Pimp, Mack and Hustler – See The Pimp Game: Instructional Guide for definitions.

Ride or Die = A Ride or Die Ho's is one who loves her pimp above all. She may or may not be the biggest risk. She is willing to sacrifice everything including her life for the cause. But it works like a seesaw. She is as loyal to her pimp as her pimp is to her. Ride or Die means "Either I'm riding with you or I'm dead. No other option." Her loyalty must be reciprocated, or she will become a pimp's worst nightmare. She may or may not be his Bottom Woman.

Man of Respect = This term is used to describe a made member of the Italian Mafia. 'I've dealt with several 'Made Guys' and I've never heard them use the words Mafia or Goodfella. I have heard the term "Wise Guy" to describe a low-level member (soldier) or a connected guy.

Lounge = A Lounge is similar to an After Hours but not the same. If the After Hours is a club a lounge would be the V.I.P. section. A lounge has prostitutes, alcohol and low playing music. They're may be drugs there such as marijuana and powder cocaine but none of the heavy stuff (crack, meth, heroin). People are seated on couches and the patrons are hand selected.

Star = The Ho who brings in the most money consistently is referred to as your star (or thorough bread). She's not the captain of the team but she is the highest scorer. She is a cut above the rest. A pimp with a Star must be careful not to devote more time and effort to the Star thus making the other

Ho's jealous. That could bring the entire house of cards crashing down and leave him with no Ho's except your Star thus demoting your status from C.E.O. Pimp to Romeo Pimp.

Ten Toes Down = The term 'Ten Toes Down' has replaced the former term 'Track Star.' The term Ten Toes refer to the feet. This is a Ho who has no problem walking the track. Most Hos are uncomfortable walking the track or working the corner.

Hooker = A prostitute with a pimp. A term that has been replaced in recent years with the term 'ho' because it's the slang version of the word whore. A whore is derogatory term for prostitute.

Renegade = A prostitute working without the assistance of a pimp or madam.

Ho = A prostitute or it could be used to label a woman who's sexually promiscuous but not a prostitute. It's the Ebonics translation for the word 'whore.'

Crack Ho = A prostitute on major drugs (crack, meth, heroin). Her cost is cheap (5 – 20 dollars) and her service is lousy and usually rushed.

Call Girl = A Call Girl is a prostitute that works by appointment only. She doesn't walk the track. She doesn't strip. She does in call and out call. She gets her clients via advertisement or through a pimp, madam, or escort service. Her clients are pre-screened, and she works with a bodyguard/driver. She is essentially an independent contractor who pays for transportation, security and broker fees. She relies on repeat business because she doesn't get the volume of request that a typical prostitute would. Since she doesn't get the volume, her customer service has to be impeccable. Her prices are higher than an 'average hooker' but her clients don't mind paying extra for the great service and her discretionary personal touch.

Escort = The acceptable present term for Call Girl.

Lady of Leisure = The proper term people in the Game use to call prostitutes. It's non-derogatory. That's the term in which they use to describe themselves.

Mistress = This term has two meanings:
1) Side chick who is being financially supported by a married man or Sugardaddy. She is not a prostitute per say. She is one man's personal sex partner but not their main love interest.
2) The proper title used for an adult entertainer or Call Girl who specializes in B.D.S.M. (Bondage, Dominatrix, Sadomasochism). She is on-call and by appointment only. What differentiates her from a Call Girl are the services she provides. She's a specialist in Dom (Dominatrix) or Sub (Submissive). She specializes in pain and humiliation as a Dom.
As a Sub, she caters to the sadism in her clients.

The Dominatrix/Mistress usually has a long-term professional relationship with her masochistic clients.

The Track = The track is the selected section of streets in a particular city that's widely known for prostitution. The prostitutes stand outside on the corners of these streets or walk back and forth within the selected section in hopes to get a Date.

Sugarbaby = A young lady who has a Sugar Daddy.

Gigolo = A male prostitute. He is on-call like a Call Girl or escort.

Mister = A male mistress who has a Sugar Mama or one wealthy female client exclusively.

Master = Is a B.D.S.M. term used for a male dominatrix who has masochistic clients.

Fresh Fish = a new prostitute who hasn't had her first 'Date' yet.

Sugar Mama = The female equivalent of a Sugardaddy.

Cougar = an older woman who prefers younger men or women. The term Cougar comes from the fact that she doesn't wait to be chosen. She is the aggressive hunter.

Slut = A promiscuous women who has sex with

multiple partners for free.

Out of Pocket = This term refers mostly to a prostitute who is being disrespectful or disobedient to her pimp or wife-in-laws.

The Underworld = The Underworld runs parallel to the Shadow World. Drug Dealers, Loan Sharks, Bookies, Hit Men, Mafioso's, Con Men, Organized Crime figures are all a part of the Underworld. The reason the Shadow World and Underworld both use the suffix 'world' because they both have rules and regulations, taxes, judges, jury's and executioners, structure, hierarchy, crime and punishment etc.

Drug Dealer = A person who buys and sells drugs, manufacture, wholesalers, distributors and retailers of drugs all fall under this heading, label or category.

Mule = The lowest level in the drug business and the highest risk. A drug mule is a man/woman who picks up large amounts of drugs from one place and delivers large amounts of drugs to another. Sometimes the drugs are packed literally in his/her body.

Middleman = In the drug business the middleman connects the suppliers with the distributor/wholesalers, or they connect the distributors/wholesalers to the retailers. He is often called a "Go-Between" or "Connect".
He collects a fee for every connection he makes.

<u>Kingpin</u> = A large drug dealer who is so large where he can actually supply the street dealers from the source. He is usually a wholesaler who supplies drug dealers. He is known for not sharing the spoils of his empire with his employees but keeping most profits for himself. This very fact is why the average Kingpin's reign is 5 years or less.

<u>Muscle</u> = In the Shadow World and or Underworld, the muscle is a driver, bodyguard, part-time low-level Hitman, and or debt collector.

<u>Overlord</u> = An Overlord is a drug dealer who only deals with Kingpins and drug lords making him an Overlord. An overlord is the manufacture who only fills huge orders from distributors and wholesalers.

<u>Drug Lord</u> = A wholesaler who supplies multiple King Pins with drugs.

<u>Drug Pusher</u> = A drug dealer who doesn't have a regular clientele so instead of a steady consumer market at his disposal, he has to persuade new customers to buy from him and or aggressively create new addicts. Pushing the drug onto unsuspecting naive.

<u>Corner Man</u> = A low level street drug dealer who deals with addicts' hand to hand,

<u>Loan Shark</u> = An organized crime figure who acts as a bank to criminals and select non-affiliated

persons. He loans money at 3 – 15% weekly interest. The only way to pay him off is by paying the entire loan back at one time in full.

Hitman = A contract killer. One who engages in murder for hire. To be a successful Hitman, you need several things:
1) Urban and combat guerilla warfare. Hand to hand combat.
2) Access to a wide range of weapons (guns, knives, crossbows, and explosives and poisons).
3) Be multi Dimensions. A hitman isn't muscle (hired gun). He's an execution specialist.
4) Ability to get the job done no matter how gruesome without conscience coming into play.
5) For a Steady stream of work, you'll need a broker (Organized crime, drug dealers, corporate moguls, entertainers). I use the term "Hitman" for identity purposes, but I've never heard Hitmen refer to themselves that way. I've heard them referred to as "He's reliable" or "He ties up loose ends". "Putting in work." Hitmen refer to their past targets as "A Job" or "Work". He may have a business card that reads 'Security Specialist, all jobs considered' or "Private Security Consultant."

Bookie = A bookmaker whom the public place sports bets with. He collects the money and covers the bets. He often works in unison with a Loan Shark.

Trick = A client of a prostitute.
Turned Out = When a pimp transforms a woman

into a prostitute.

Incall = A term used in the game when a trick dates a hooker at her location, by appointment only.

Outcall = A term used in the game when a trick dates a hooker at his location.

Captain Save A Hoe = A trick who falls in love with a hooker or stripper then tries to persuade her to quit her profession and become his wife or girlfriend.

Misogynistic Sadist = He is the biggest threat to a Ho. He hates women in general and wants to punish them by humiliating, harming and in some cases killing them.

The Square = A person or term used for a civilian. One who is neither a member of the Underworld nor Shadow World.

Rules and Regulations = The guidelines for the Pimp Game and or the Pimps individual Do's and Don'ts when it comes to his stable.

Chapter 5
Sharpening the Sword

It's a lot to digest all at once. Most people are unaware that these parallel worlds even exist. The response I've grown accustomed to is shock. But for those of us who exist in these worlds we are un-shockable. The things I've seen and done would make a Vietnam Veteran squeamish.

For career criminals, jail and prison serve as a frat house. In the Underworld, prison is referred to as 'College.' In the Shadow World, prison is referred to as 'Vacation.' As I grew older, I understood why. It's only three things to do in the Penitentiary:

1) Become a new person.
2) Rest and relax.
3) Become a better criminal.

At different times in my life I've done all three. As a youth between the ages of 13 – 18.

I was known as someone who would stop your oxygen in a heartbeat (no pun intended). In my mid 20's, I was known as a good earner. Someone who could make my something out of nothing. In my 30's, I was known for my cult-like loyalty to those under my umbrella of protection.

Currently in my early 40's, I'm known for and respected for all three. In this life a good reputation takes a lifetime to build and solidify and just one wrong transaction to destroy. My reputation is rock solid. If it were not, I would have been dead decades ago.

I've seen grown men cry like newborn babies after leaving court and hearing, "Life without the possibility of parole." I've lived through prison riots, gun shots, conspiracy's police frame ups, and more fights than you have fingers and toes. We as human beings make this beautiful non-redeemable gift of life, this one-way journey so painful for one another. But I digress.

Image in the life is very important. You naturally develop a style and strut based on your persona. That's known as 'Felling yourself." To live this life, you must have a strong sense of self. Reason being because that's who you'll be spending the majority of your time with yourself.

Vampires (pimps) don't travel in packs. You're always being watched so be knowledgeable and aware of your surroundings. You're also always being judged. The Game like any game has a hierarchy, In the Shadow World as well as the underworld.

Rules and regulations must be observed and followed. These worlds are as real as real can get. Because of my gangster roots, I reacted and responded to issues in the Shadow World with an Underworld style.

I didn't know at the time in my mid 20's that the loyalty I showed to my ladies was virtually unheard of. Since I came from a gangsta (later from a gangster) background, I actually saw my ladies as my family and treated them as such. I wasn't comfortable taking 100% of my ladies' money. That 100% sounded to me like a selfish self-centered Kingpin and I've seen the Julius Caesar's (Kingpin) come and go.

I was out to build something much stronger than a pimp's stable. My aim and goal was to unionize adult entertainers. That's what Ladies of Leisure are. Also, I felt a management fee of 35% to 50% was fair. That 50% covered security, transportation and guidance. In my early days when I was 2 or 3 wives deep, I took 100%. That's the way I was taught. But then the logically side of my brain kicked in. I figured why take 100% of 3 when I can take 50% of 25.

I had aspirations of an agency, not just an on the corner, rhyme speaking Ghetto Pimp. So, I got my women on board and I/we grew. Pimps who have the IZM spend energy and effort concealing the knowledge, wisdom and understanding of the IZM from their Ho's. Keeping them ignorant and unaware of its eye-opening power. Thus, keeping them perpetually depending on him.

I remember Gorgeous (read about her in Along for The Ride) saying "Don't exclude me, include me so I can help us." From that moment on I decided to teach and tutor my wives in the subtleties of the IZM. You don't feed a newborn baby steak. Once they gasped an understanding, I taught them more and more. Their understanding of the IZM increased productivity by 300 plus percent.

Keep in mind in the United States during the 1800's Cotton production increased by almost 300% under the share cropping than slavery. If you want workers to take pride in ownership you'll have to first, make them owners.

It was that decision to go against years of tradition and apply common sense fair tactics that put my name on the tongue of every Ho in the street. My reputation grew and pushed me right into the pornography business.

Here was yet another avenue in which my wives could blossom and flourish. It meant more money for me and for them as well. I wanted my wives to be a cut above the rest and to do this I needed them to be the smartest ladies in the game. One thing about knowledge. The more you learn the more you hunger for more.

The IZM is an ever-growing source of unlimited power. A wise man Michael Esposito told me "An Army travels on its stomach. If you can't feed them, then you can't lead them." For those reasons, I pay my people first and myself last. Anything worth doing is worth doing right. Before you practice or preform a trapeze act no matter how skilled you are you must secure the safety net first.

You don't plan to fail, but if you have a safety net, you can secure a second chance. Condoms, seatbelts and helmets save lives. When entering a criminal ventured you apply the exact same principles.

I found a great criminal defense lawyer. I researched his record and saw that he had experience with getting high profiled infamous clients much needed "Not guilty" verdicts. I met with him and paid a retainer. I explained to him to answer my collect calls. If I don't require his services within one full calendar year the retainer in his. At that point I would pay another retainer with a 365-expiration date. He agreed.

I then a found the bail bondsman with the best rates. I developed a rapport with him. I didn't leave a deposit, but I got his card. I began writing personal checks made out to the "P.A.L" Police Activities League. That was to build a consistent paper trail. I put up 60% of my cash stash in my bank's safety deposit box. I installed a land line (phone line) in my office and bought a pager. Why? Because they can't be GPS tracked like cell phones. Also, land line phones require a court order to tap, cell phones don't.

I never discussed business on the phone anyway, or any phone for that matter. These parameters were basic safety measures. That way if one or more of my wives were locked up, I could get them out within hours. The ladies know not to call me from there cell phones or a jail phone. They'd go to my office and use the office phone to page me.

Just in case my phone records are subpoenaed. The wives would commit our 'family attorney's number to memory.

They were to call him and give the code over the phone. The code was "A.R" which meant "Advance Retainer." I would receive a page and call the lawyer form a phone booth 20 minutes away. If I could bail her out, I took the lawyer the money to bond her out. By chance if she was on probation or parole and had an 'N' status meaning no bail is available, I'd max out her books. The limit an inmate can have on their books is $999.00 (max out).

The lawyer would personally put the money on her books out of the deposit I gave. The lawyer and my relationship to him is protected under attorney client privilege. I'd pay in cash only. My power and protection lie in my anonymity. I'd then call a Royal Family meeting and enforce rules regulations under incarceration as follows:

The wives and I were on a 60/40 split. That's only if were 5 or more wives deep. If less, than 5, it's a 55/45 split both in their favor. If I had 6 wives and one went to jail, the split is altered to accommodate our fallen mistress. Each lady puts up 5% of their weekly earnings to be collected by me every week. The fallen mistress/wife will collect for example: Each wife pulls in 500 a day, net 300 for her that's 1800.00 in a 6-day work week net. 5% of 1,800 is 90.00 x 5= 450.00. This continues until our "Soldierette" is home. Since she was unable to produce an income for herself, the Royal Family still provided a suitable consolation prize for her.

This lets her know she is loved and appreciated. That's unionized regulated prostitution. That's the "Mickey-way." When you have a reputation of being firm and fair recruitment becomes a non-factor. I soon had over 30 at one time (at my height of the game) in 5 houses in select locations. 100% from 5 wives or 50% from 30 wives. You do the math. We all get rich.

If a wife brought me a new lady and she passes my examination and probationary period, the wife that brought her gets 10% of her earnings on a bonus check. That's 10% per week as long as she's a Royal Family member. Everyone felt safe and secure.

I was never arrested or even questioned for pandering, pimping, white slavery, kidnapping or human trafficking. There had never been a rat (snitch) in my stables. My arrest came from acts of violence protecting my wives, not hurting or harming my wives in anyway.

In the Underworld a Made Guy introduced another Made Guy as 'a Friend of Ours' to other Made Guys. In the Shadow World one Mack or Pimp introduces another Mack or Pimp as a 'Gentleman.'

My wives' nature, speech, attitude and charisma are all reflections of myself and standards. My work weeks were usually 5 days, not seven. I gave each woman 2 weeks paid vacation, sick time, maternity leave (with us contributing 5% as if she were in jail). Starting after the first trimester. We filed taxes 1099 independent contractors under a blanket LLC.

But to have it this tight wasn't by no way an overnight journey. Once I adopted the IZM as the true way of life, I became free. Even at times 'behind the wall' (prison) I feel 100% free. As I've educated my wives in the subtleties of the IZM, they've found eternal peace on this earth.

It's like going to heaven but not having to die. The tree of knowledge, the branches of wisdom, and the fruit of understanding growing freely out of the garden of you. It's not that I'm a law breaker. I just don't acknowledge any man-made laws.

I follow the laws of the universe in which we were all created and must obey. I say what I want, and I do what I please. I laugh at 'Normies' who are so controllable to the point that they believe that a fiery pit awaits them underground with a red man and pitchfork. That sounds like the author of that fairy tale was on LSD.

Tell me this; When a lion murders a zebra, is that lion going to Hell? Is that lion going to prison? To actually witness this, you would even be shocked. Well, I see myself as a lion and the entire homo-sapien species as zebras, so graze carefully. But you've adopted these man-made systems as rules to live by.

You conform to illogical doctrines in hopes that the authors of these brainwashing zombie making systems will look favorably upon you and allow you to accumulate green pieces of paper with his picture on it so you can exchange dirty green papers for trinkets. So pathetic the homo-sapien is.

The IZM will make you a God among insects. That's why mentors and teachers are so important and should be chosen wisely. If you don't put it in, then you can't pull it out. What a terrible life to live if in servitude to another. For reasons such as that, is the reason I was uncomfortable taking 100%. I started that way because that's the way I was taught. But like with anything, you have to put your own methods of operation into your program. If you walk in another man's footsteps it will only lead you to where someone else has already been. You have to make your own footsteps in the snow.

Walk a different path, walk in the light of logic. I learned a lot in the way of mysticism from Osiris. He spent countless hours meditating in a sleep deprivation tank he kept in his bedroom.

He was a bit of a miser. I had seen him go into his wall safe on several occasions. He had anywhere from 60 to 80 Grand in stacks of 10 thousand. He drove an old Subaru hatch back. He had a Lincoln Town car he only pulled out of the garage when he had a meeting to attend. His furniture was old. The kind you'd fine in an antique store. His modest 2-bedroom home smelled like Ben Gay.

He lived alone and almost never had company. He played chess and dominoes (only with me). He was extremely stand offish and antisocial. He didn't seem to trust anyone but me. I never met or mentioned his daughter. I didn't feel it was my place to. He was a Vietnam Veteran. He flew helicopter during the Vietnam Conflict.

I've noticed that most of my mentors were Veterans of war. A couple of them were still dealing with P.T.S.D. intensity combined with my already Bi-polar brain made for a lethal combination. I transformed my weaknesses into strengths and my faults into attributes. All of which I did though the IZM.

Osiris had a college degree in Cultural Anthropology. He was a master in behavioral science and body language. He attended séances and was obsessed with the occult and study of mental telepathy. He was a mystic. At least in my eyes. He always said to me "When and opportunity appears through an open door, run through it before it closes."

To this day, I live by that advice. In order to learn, you must learn to un-learn what you have learned and learn to learn again. Once you adopt the IZM as your system, you'll freely develop knowledge, wisdom and understanding that will supersede all systems, thus making you more powerful then you can possibly imagine.

The IZM will unlock the inner power within you because it bypasses the man-made information of the conscious mind and logically communicates with the subconscious mind.

Have you ever taken a long time to learn something and you can learn something else immediately? The one you learned immediately was logically (mathematically) inserted. When men who have never controlled people are thrusted into a position where they control people, one has a tendency to inflate one's own sense of self-worth.

A pimp's weakness which is vanity often leads to a pimp's downfall. When I was a young lad, my mother told me that true power rest behind the throne, not on it. I stayed in the shadows only to reveal myself when it was time. Time dictates my agenda. If I were currently in the game, the last thing I would be doing is writing books.

Phil Jackson can't play for the Los Angeles Lakers and coach them simultaneously. I closed a chapter in my life in order to open another one. I've heard pimps on interviews say that a prostitute chooses them. They've said a Ho has to already be a Ho in the game. That a pimp can't make a square woman a Ho. That's 100% false.

You can make a king a slave, a schoolteacher a porn star, a gangster a minister, a virgin a prostitute. One of the most alluring things about the human mind and humanity in general is its ability to change in stages. The ability to transform one's thoughts process can alter the future.

What if Adolf Hitler had become a concert pianist instead of a dictator? That's how the future can be altered through actions in the present. It's easy to turn a virgin into a whore. Just as easy as it is to turn a convicted killer into a minister, through desire and desired actions.

The wills of men and women have been controlled since the beginning of men and women. The same way the government of the United States convince my father at the age of 20 to enlist in the Army and run off to combat in Vietnam? Turning out is a process that can't ever be done twice.

Once a woman had been 'turned out' they can only be 'turned on' or 'turned off'' from that moment. The reason's those pimps made those statements is because their ego's come into play, "If I can't do it, then it's impossible." What they should have said "My IZM just isn't on that level yet." At least they would have been honest. That statement would have been befittingly accurate. As with any science there are levels of consciousness. Degrees of enlightenment which may end up developing a sense of entitlement. Be warned.

If you're not on a particular level, don't assume that level hasn't been reached by someone else. A famous player from Chicago named International Lucky once told me that he had met a woman who worked in a bank. A month later she was walking the track in front of the bank she previously worked at a teller.

I've turned on and have turned out. It's much easier turning on. To get a Ho on your team who had previously been with a pimp is easiest. She has already been turned out. You need not test her. Just go over your particular rules and regulations then send her. If she's with a pimp and you 'turn her on' to you and she comes to join your stable, then you've knocked that pimp. If a woman is a square and after experiencing your IZM wished to join your stable as a Ho, then she's been turned out.

To turn a woman out or lead or mislead a person locate their desires, grab a hold of them or the map to them, then lead the Ho where you want them to go.

Force the mirror test. Introduce her to all that comes with your life/lifestyle then sentence her to her own life. She'll beg you for parole. Webster's dictionary's definition for sin is; Sin – "A breaking of a law enforced by a religion." Not necessarily God, but man-made religions.

Homo-sapiens who are envious of God's power often attempt to align themselves with God's power by doing what they call 'His work'. If he's God, then your help would be useless and futile. Religion's use God and ancient text as a way to justify their cruelty and self-serving agenda. It's painfully obvious.

Sins and the indecisive guilt that follows are deeply rooted in controllable characteristics within the human subconscious. Characteristics that came pre-loaded before birth. They aren't taught by man, but they are fertilized, nurtured and developed by man ofttimes without being conscious of the fact.

According to Christian folklore, Adam and Eve hat two children, Cain and Able. Cain was jealous of Able and killed him. He wasn't taught jealousy nor murder from any outside source or influence. Hidden deep within the human psyche lies great power and unexplainable phenomena. Since the mind is set to self-preservation innately, the subconscious will only summons these powers in life or death situations.

What if these powers can be unlocked with a key fashioned by the conscious mind? What if I told you that you'll be able to use this fashioned key to unlock your abilities whenever you wanted without a life of death situation? This question has been raised by both religion and science alike. In a deep state of meditation, I am able to freeze each side of my brain, one side at a time.

My conscience mind will take precise detailed pinpointed steps while it explores the frozen subconscious mind. Then the subconscious will make a sweeping analysis of the frozen conscious mind to locate the locked section and open it.

This takes years of practice and can be physically painful. In my youth, there was a television show that I use to beg my parents to let me stay up past my bedtime and watch. It was called 'The Incredible Hulk' starring Bill Bixby as David Bruce Banner and Lou Ferrigno as the Hulk. The introduction of the show goes as follows; "Dr David Banner, physician, scientist, looking to tap into the hidden strength that all humans have."

Where did Dr. David Banner go looking for this hidden strength? In the human body? No, he went looking into the human mind. Why? Because he knew it was already there. He didn't create it. He went looking for it. He didn't put it there, but he knew that's where it was. If he didn't put it there, then his brain must have had it pre-loaded prior to his birth while he was being fashioned in the womb.

Endorphins, serotonin, dimethyltryptamine and adrenaline etc. we'll dive into at a later date for an in-depth lesson. Google those four words, learn their meanings and what effect they have on the human mind. That's where we will begin the next 'Pimp Game' lesson. There are triggers in the brain that if activated, can unlock and unleash these hidden strengths. Example;

I was arrested on a very serious charge when I was in my early 20's. At the arraignment, the judge read the charges. Then he announced what the maximum penalty was if I were to lose my case. I didn't hear anything he said but 25 to life. I stopped breathing and began violently coughing. The judge instructed my lawyer to explain to me that I was not being sentenced, then he ordered the bailiff to fetch me a glass of water.

When I heard 25 to life, my heart skipped a beat and my knees gave out. I couldn't stand or breath. All the judge said were 4 words, '25 to life' and my mood was affected. My mood sent a distress signal to my body and it was also affected. The judge didn't shoot me in the legs with a shotgun, but my legs gave out.

So, if a person can affect someone's mood with words and someone's mood can affect their body internally and conscious actions. Then a person's words can control someone's body and actions. A+B=C, A+D=C, B=D. Knowing when to use these powers of persuasions takes optical and auditory literacy. Listening for clues. Deciphering body language, transforming intensions to a mathematical equation, solving for X and reading between the lines.

Ink Blotch: When I was 13, my parents sent me to what would be my first psychiatrist. I was nervous at first, so he asked me to talk. When I asked him, what should I talk about? He answered, "Anything you'd like." As I began to speak, he started to write.

After only five minutes of talking, he asked me to look at these shadowy black pictures on white papers and say what I saw. He told me to say the first thing that popped into my head. We went from slide to slide and through multi-interpretations of what I saw as he wrote. The psychiatrist was writing my thoughts so later he could read my mind.

These weren't photos of anything in particular. They were just stains of ink on a white surface resembling a Jackson Pollock painting. My answers were based on my perceptions. My perceptions were based on my experiences and preconceived thoughts. Saying the first things that came to mind didn't give my conscious mind enough time to process the information.

Instead, my subconscious was forced to respond by reflex based on stored information. The ability to sensor is a characteristic solely given to the conscious mind. Example: Have you ever been faced with a decision and immediately come up with an answer? Then talk yourself out of that answer, and decided to go with another answer? Only to find out your original answer was correct, and you said, "I should have followed my first mind?"

Your first mind, your subconscious, doesn't possess the ability to ponder, create anxiety, then allow those feelings to alter or influence decisions. Doubt is a trait only the conscious mind possesses. When you second guess yourself, that's the conscious mind over-riding a command given by your subconscious. The subconscious doesn't have the ability break the law of self-preservation.

Chapter 6
Seven Deadly Sins – Sloth, Envy, Greed, Pride, Lust, Vanity and Wrath.

1. Sloth – Laziness

2. Envy – Discontent aroused by another's possessions or qualities, with a strong desire to have them for one's self.

3. Greed – Rapacious desire, avarice.

4. Pride – Self-respect. 2. Satisfaction over one's accomplishments or possessions. 3. A cause or source of this. 4. Conceit, arrogance. 5. A group of lions.

5. Lust – 1. Sexual craving. 2. Any overwhelming craving. 3. To have an inordinate desire.

6. Vanity - Excessive pride, conceit.

7. Wrath – Violent, resentful anger. 2. Retribution.

All seven have a connection with one dangerous thing in common. What possible link could there be for these seven seemingly non-related attributes? All seven of these forces have the uncanny ability to override the subconscious mind and block any messages stimming from the conscious mind.

This happens in a fraction of a second. When that happens, one or several of those forces are in complete control of your thoughts and actions. Because it happens so quickly, it's gotten its name from the speed in which it happens, "SNAP."

Snap or Snapping is such an excepted psychological term by mainstream society. That's why when you regain control via your conscious or subconscious mind it's referred to as "Snapping out of it." Snapping out of it is commonly used when someone is coming out of a trance. A trance in which they were not in complete control. Legally, it's referred to as "Temporary Insanity."

If lawyers and judges accept this 'trance' as a synonym meaning temporary insanity, then the characteristics of this trance must make its host crazy. Or as it's commonly put, he/she wasn't in his/her "Right Mind." Or "Right State of Mind." You may hear it put both ways.

As a man who lives everyday with Bi-polar Disorder, I fully understand snapping. One could say I have a vested interest in the inner workings of the human psyche. If you're able to summons one or more of these Seven Sins in a person that would give you unlimited power.

Example: Adolf Hitler, Jesus Christ, The Dali Lama, Jim Jones, Dr. Martin Luther King, Elijah Muhammad, Vince Lombardi etc. I could go on forever but I'm sure you've absorbed the point. The use of one or more of the Seven Deadly Sins is a powerful weapon and a strong predecessor for the mastering of 'Strands' and 'Receptors.'

When someone is in this state of mind, its ofttimes referred to as 'Losing Control.' I've heard most of these 7 forces as being in a state of blindness. Example: He was blinded by Greed. Remember the movie 'The Bodyguard' starring Whitney Houston? Her sister in the movie was blinded by Envy and also driven by Wrath. By the time she "Snapped out of it" it was too late. Sloth is in a class all by its powerful self. Because sloth shuts down all production.

Any of the seven can prove damaging and or fatal for its host. Since everything is controlled by the mind, then the mind is the ONLY thing worth controlling. There are many roads that lead to that destination.

The in-depth obsession with cultural anthropology which I have because of Osiris lead me into behavioral science. My research lead me to several countries around the world and right back here.

The knowledge, wisdom and understanding are to be used in the world that surrounds you! Upon my 'Awakening,' I immediately implemented my neurological powers into the world I was in. The Underworld. My mastery and Gorgeous (read about her in my novel

Along for the Ride) lead me into the Shadow
World. That's where I dwell.
Where do you dwell? My aim is not to
transform you into a pimp. My aim is to transform
you into a master among slaves, in YOUR world,
not in mines. Thus, the reason the transformational
literature must be logically(mathematically)
uploaded. That makes it universally transferable.
Its universal transferability is what makes the IZM
priceless.
I teach skills and tactics from the source,
the mind. Always remember the kiosk. You can use
your powers wherever you go, whenever you like.
You can also use your powers without even being
present. We'll go into that during Strands,
Receptors and Seeds. You possess the power to
expand your realm. It's up to you what world you
apply it to. So, aim high.
A street pimp is the lowest form to wheel
the IZM. Wheel it as a preacher or politician, an
entrepreneur, businessman or women. It's much too
potent for such low endeavors. I was blessed with
the IZM at a young age. When I ate the forbidden
fruit from The Tree of Knowledge, I was just a
teenager.
I applied my powers and skill to the world I
was currently in, which were the mean streets of
South-Central Los Angeles. please never think you
have to use the IZM in my realm. And never
shortchange your ambition and over-think yourself
off the road less traveled by. The best thing about
the IZM is no matter if it's kiosk size or the size of
planet Earth, The IZM does not dilute as it expands.

If you have 2 subjects or 200 subjects the IZM will accommodate evenly equally. The size of your realm is entirely up to you. Understand, because if its mathematical logic the IZM's power is not gender based. You can be man or woman. All you need is a brain and functional central nervous system. Neurology is not gender based. Size has never mattered in cases that do not involve direct measurable comparisons. The size and strength of your tree depends on how you feed and cultivate it. If the apple tree is 50ft tall, how would one pluck the fruit? Grow to your specifications that best suits you currently. But remember to leave room for growth (expansion). And always have an exit plan. Leave yourself an out. What's a building without emergency exits? A large coffin.

That analogy is figurately transferable. Since "we're born in sin" as the scriptures say, many take this to mean sex is a sin. Or humans are conceived out of an act of sin. That's why I say I have no problem with religion, but a serious problem with man's interpretation of it. Through man's limited understanding of ancient scribes, he has caused more bloodshed in the name of brotherhood. More wars, in the name of peace. More hatred, motivated by his so-called love. Homosapiens are a foolish species.

When I was 17 in the 11th grade I wrote a term paper intitled "Human Beings: God's Only Mistake." I can remember my stunned classmates expressions as I read it. I backed my accusations with hard facts. In man's limited, dogmatic self-serving understanding he has successfully warped opinions based on inaccurate interpretations.

The reason the ancient text says "we're all born in (not of) sin" doesn't point to how we're born (sexually), but what we're born with. That which is innately in us, that was formulated in the womb. That which we weren't taught, but somehow know. What sin or sins could an infant be born with? What sin could possibly be so innately deep, that homosapiens are unaware of? If a sin or anything else is innately in us and no one taught it to us, then it is located in the subconscious mind.

What sins were we born with? Or traits indicating seeds (sins in embryonic states) that need only fertilizer to grow. A catalyst if you will. Slothfulness, Envy, Greed, Pride, Lust, Vanity and Wrath/Rage are not taught. We're born with these character traits deep within our subconscious. Love, Trust, Loyalty, Humility, Discipline, Sacrifice and Steadfastness are character traits humans are not born with but taught and developed. These must be uploaded by the conscious mind via our 5 senses and practiced until it's accepted by the subconscious mind.

At that point it's called routine. Hence the term 'Build Character.' Which implies conscious thought and direction. Once repetition from the conscious mind had been made routine by the subconscious mind it goes into phase three, 'reflex. Reflex is something done without assistance from the conscious mind.

Reflex is the highest form of acceptance the subconscious mind gives. It earns a new title, 'instinctive.' Instinct is when the subconscious is in complete control. When the subconscious is in complete control it eliminates all forms of processing. When processing is eliminated then so too is the time processing takes, such elimination of allotted time increases the speed instincts use.

Example: When I trained in boxing and the martial arts, I noticed common treads between them, repetition. It's a long, tedious task of doing the same thing over and over. The conscious mind preforms these tasks throughout its journey until it reaches its destination. The journey is as follows, conscious mind repetition. Overtime it becomes routine (still in the conscious mind). From routine, the subconscious mind accepts it. From the subconscious, that repetition becomes reflex. You'll preform reflex 'without thinking.'

Karate has 12 basic movements. 4 blocks, 4 kicks and 4 punches, that's it. You learn all 12 the first day. From then on out you'll train these 12 movements until it becomes reflex. How you combinate these 12 movements will determine your rate of advancement

The scripture should read "We are all born with sin." It would have a better chance of correct interpretation than "We are all born in sin." If the scripture read "We are all born into sin" that would imply that the world around us (that a newborn didn't create) are sinners.

The stressing of one vowel over another, or the absence of a word or phrase can change the meaning entirely. Thus, altering its interpretation. That's the main reason man is lost. He's reading the map wrong. His misinterpretation of ancient script has him searching in the wrong place. Interpretation is as important as the text itself. Read these sentences which will appear to be the exact same but possess very different meanings. Example: stress the underlined word.

1.They asked you to coach <u>Football</u>? Implies that's not your desired sport of expertise.

2. They asked you to <u>Coach</u> football? Implies that you would be better suited as a player or another position of that program.

3. They asked <u>You</u> to coach football? Implies that you're not qualified for the job.

4. They <u>Asked</u> you to coach football? Implies that the question itself was rhetorical. Or it implies that you really don't have a choice but to.

The same sentence written the exact same way with completely different meanings. If not of the underlined words to indicate which word to stress it is easy to see how this message, if delivered by text, could become lost in translation. In short man is clueless and that's putting it lightly.

Chapter 7
Receptors, Strands and Seeds

Understanding mind control and how to use it requires a thorough in-depth knowledge. Mastery is only achieved after reaching the inner core-link of knowledge, wisdom and understanding of the total complexity of the IZM. In previous chapters, the Seven Deadly Sins were discussed. The power they possess if unleashed, in practicing mind control they are even stronger weapons at your disposal. There are deeper powers with the sinister aura of omnipotence. When someone is being manipulated by someone else using one or more of the Seven Deadly Sins against him, the subject is powerless to resist.

Have you noticed how easy it is to chew and swallow candy? Have you noticed how hard it is to chew and swallow gum? The body follows orders you give it to the best of its ability.

The conscious and the subconscious mind are in agreement on the act of chewing food into small enough pieces to be swallowed smoothly. The subconscious mind has accepted the rule of chewing gum and refraining from swallowing.

In order to swallow the gum, the conscious mind must over-ride the order from the subconscious mind. This requires complete concentration on the part of the conscious mind and reluctant submission from the subconscious mind. Such an over-ride could be met with conflict from the subconscious mind but ultimately submitting to the will of the conscious mind.

The rest of the body doesn't get the 'over-ride' memo in time. During such an over-ride, the subject may bite his/her tongue or even choke. Receptors: What are they and how do they work? Much like the Seven Deadly Sins, we are all born with Receptors. An example of Receptors; Love, Hate, Jealousy, all 7 Sins, Affirmation, Acceptance, etc. Natural motivators within the human psyche. Remember; The only thing that motivates any living organism is one of two things;
1. To seek a possible gain.
2. To avoid a possible loss.

If presented with 1 or 2 or both you can maneuver humans as if you were manipulating them with a remote control. This scenario will bring your chess game to life. It's a far advanced version of the Carrot, the Horse and Cart. The phrase "Touched a Nerve" or "Tickled a Nerve" refers to receptors. Receptors are those nerves. Some are thicker, stronger and longer than others, but rest assured,

they are all in there, with a few acceptations.
These Receptors effect every facet of the brain in one way or another. Once someone told me that I have a very low fear receptor. He also said that I would have to bungee jump or play Russian Roulette to experience the same amount of thrill a normal person would from a bite of chocolate. Or buying a new pair of shoes.

Receptors give off signals, but their primary function is to receive signals and transmit those signals to the brain. The brain uses receptors in communicating like Red Ants use their antennas for communication. When I first discovered receptors, I began using my newfound skill to make money. I cleaned up in No Limit Hold'em poker games. Receptors are 'tells' that the brain can't hide.

Whatever the brain is thinking, the receptors will show. All you have to do is be able to read them. Some people possess low pain receptors (daredevils, pro Boxers, football players). To judge the length of someone's receptors you have to phish for clues. As I explained in the Pimp Game; Instructional Guide, you're sliding your hand across a brick looking for an opening, a crack.

Example: Godfather One (the movie). Don Vito Corleone was having a 'sit down' (meeting) with Sollozzo the Turk. Every offer the Turk made, Don Corleone refused. The Turk was searching for a Receptor. An opening he could enter. The Turk was smart. He tried three different receptors during this meeting (chess match of wit and wills). The Turk first appealed to his greed but to no avail. Then he appealed to his pride, in submission to the

Don's power. Lastly, sensing the Don's fear of risk (if the Don entered the drug business, he may lose his political friends. The Don's source of sustaining his position of power lies in his vast number of political friends).

The Turk told the Don that the Tattaglia Family would provide security and insurance for the Don's investment. As the Don was explaining why his answer was still no, the Don's son, Sonny Corleone expressed interest in The Turk deals and wanted to hear more. The Turk touched a nerve. The Corleone family revealed a crack, an opening. They were not a united front as they appeared. That one interruption by Sonny lead to the Turk arranging the Don's assassination attempt.

The Turk's plan was to make the deal with Sonny. When the Turk left, the Don told his son Sonny "Never let anyone outside the family know what you're thinking again." The Don implied that the Turk could read Sonny's mind because of what Sonny said, how he said it, his body language and when Sonny interrupted the conversation. In that one instant Sonny closed his father's casket without possessing a clue.

RECEPTORS

To gauge Receptors, one may go phishing. This is done with buzz words or lead sentences and questions. Reading receptors doesn't require verbal interaction. An exchange of words isn't always necessary. Their body language will reveal as much

about what's on their minds as actual words would
In the movie 'Silence of the Lambs,' Hannibal Lecter played by Sir Anthony Hopkins used his powers of Receptors. Perception and deductive reasoning were used to analyze and dissect Jodi Foster within minutes. I was told by Osiris "If you sit by the river long enough, you'll see the bodies of your enemies floating by." I truly didn't understand what that meant until a decade after his death.

I was able to pick up from that understanding and continue to build. Thus, proving another thing Osiris told me "I will continue to teach and expand your knowledge, wisdom and understanding of the IZM long after my death." He was correct. But how? Remember all humans are born with receptors.

Receptors vary in length. The Seven Deadly Sins are all Receptors. You have Love, Sympathy, Empathy, etc. which lead to actions. The main precursors of the manipulation of Receptors are advertisers. When I was a child, I remember my uncle and aunt having a conversation in the kitchen about subliminal messages. Advertisers use Receptor buzz words, then Seed, all subliminal in order for you to not only do what the advertisers want. But also make you think it was your idea.

Example: Past midnight, when you are semi-conscience and your defenses (pessimism, doubts) are down, you will see an increase of television commercials about abused animals and starving children. When I was a kid I remember seeing 'Save the Whales' commercials. I remember

Jerry Lewis telethons where people would call in and pledge money. At night is when most humans choose to sleep.

The advertisers tickle the sympathy Receptors during the first part of the commercial (feeding hungry children). They'd show children in pain to get your attention. The middle of the commercial discusses the average cost of feeding a child vs the average person's wasteful spending. As you become angry from the children's lack of support, lastly the commercial informs you of how you can help.

The commercial in 60 seconds touched your sympathy Receptor, financial logic and your angry Receptor followed by your kindness Receptor to provoke response. The sympathy, logic and kindness Receptors alone aren't enough to motivate your conscious mind into action. The logic spoke to the subconscious mind. The anger(wrath) needs but a whisper to be summonsed into action. The desired response is expected. Use the correct bait and you'll catch the right fish. The consequence from action is minor in comparison to the guilt felt from complacency.

Receptors or the manipulation of, motivates action. Have you ever cheered in a movie theater? Have you ever cried at a particular part of the same movie? Were you the only one? Look to your left. Then look to your right. You were not alone. This was no coincidence. This was by design. How? the director doesn't know you all personally? By using L.C.D.'s (least common denominators). Everyone in the movie wasn't cheering or crying, but most were. L.C.D.'s cover the majority, not all. Those were examples of how receptors are tapped, tickled and or massaged on a regular basis in everyday life. By tickling, tapping or massaging the receptors brain, you're causing probable influence. Influence in only the beginning. Influence is guiding not steering. It's the power of suggestion. Suggestive influence still leaves the subject (person) with the burden of choice. As powerfully successful as subliminal messages are, the ultimate final decision is left up to the subject. But...There's a deeper...Far more powerful phantom of the ISM...Strands......

STRANDS

Strands work in unison with Receptors. Strands are manmade, pre-meditated and controlled by the conscious mind. Sinister from its core, malicious in its intent. Strands hold the power and agenda of Satanic properties. For the squeamish please do not read any further. For those of you who choose to continue... Be careful. Consider yourself... WARNED!!!

Strands and Receptors form an insidious combination of colossal proportions. The use of Strands and Receptors will put you in the mind of the Serpent. Everything you've held as innocent and pure will be no more. Together they form the forbidden fruit produced by The Tree of Knowledge (mentioned in The Book of Genesis). Nothing you see or hear will look or sound as it once did. Its transformational powers will cause a startling metamorphosis within you that will be visible to all in which you encounter. The more you use this power, the more this power uses you. It will feed upon your optimism until it consumes you. Then time will be no more but an inconsequential stitch in the fabric of life. Again ...You've been warned.

Strands...

A Strand by itself has little power. Its formed and controlled by the conscious mind for one purpose; To manipulated and control the subconscious of another. This is done when 'The Master' forms and ties a Strand to the Receptor or Receptors of his victim or victims. In my decades in mysticism, each fathom deeper than the last, I've developed sight beyond sight far beyond sight.

Foresight and insight are two separate levels of third eyesight. Through deep meditation, one can actually see Receptors and Strands as clearly as one may see the moon with their eyes. Receptors resemble antennas. Antennas stimming from the mind. They can't be destroyed or removed. They can only be strengthened, weakened and or manipulated. They can be tied, suppressed and become tangled.

Strands on the other hand can be broken, removed and or destroyed. The good news is that they usually can be repaired or reconstructed.

What are strands? If Receptors are antennas, then Strands are neurological highways in which to transmit frequencies. Visually they appear as dough. Shapeless dough which can be fashioned into a pizza, a pretzel, doughnuts etc.

You first have to construct a strand. Then you must tie your strand to your victim's Receptors. Once your Strand is tightly tied, you can send information to your subject/victim. The information you send will bypass the conscious mind and go straight to the subconscious to be absorbed as fact. This process is more commonly known as 'Brainwashing.'

Mostly this technique is practiced by religious leaders/cult leaders. When the connection is firm, the atmosphere for dogmatism will become fertile enough to plant Seeds. We will get to that later. This Strands to Receptors connection from conscious to subconscious connection is the most powerful of all. It gives the Master the keys to the vault where logic is stored. This is how cult leaders easily convince their flock to drink cyanide laced Kool-Aid.

Cult/political and religious leaders easily get men/women and place them into ovens to be burned alive. To create an entire system of subjugation only to perpetuate a race into never ending slavery.

When I was younger, I was told and taught that homicidal maniacs don't travel in groups. I was taught incorrectly. The same way one-man brainwashes one man (microcosm). That power is

merely condensed into an L.C.D., then magnified
(macrocosm) and adjusted to accommodate its
intended target.
 Example: I was phishing with a young lady
over drinks and appetizers. I made a wide range of
comments during our lightweight conversation. She
asked me if she had on too much makeup? Too
much makeup – as opposed to what? I read
insecurity and a need for affirmation from her
Receptors.
 As we spoke more, I commented on her
sister. She had begun a slight stutter. She had a
frown beginning to form. I saw where a sibling
rivalry Strand could be fashioned to fit. A need to
belong or approval Strand also, could be fashioned.
In order to tie the connections, tight enough to begin
to "brainwash" or "reprogram" her subconscious
(hard drive) I needed more cultivating.
 As she revealed more about herself, I read
more between the lines. There is truth in lies. It can
tell you more about the person than the truth their
attempting to conceal. With her, I built several
Strands. I built an approval system based on my
comments and gestures to tie up her need to belong.
She would compete with herself for my emotional
responses. Upon doing that, I had to make sure my
responses were earned and only matched with her
maximum efforts.
 The dog must do a trick for a treat. I knew
her sister was a sore spot for her, so I merely
touched it ever so slightly, occasionally to distract
from the fact that I was building another Strand.
The need for approval always takes a person

momentarily out of their comfort zone.

In order for the subject/victim with a 'need for approval' can get back on solid ground you'd create a Strand to whereas the system of values is based on the subject's individual characteristics. By doing that it will transform her faults into attributes. In order to be physically out of sight to remain the driver of your subject's antenna's, the dropping of "Seeds" are a great method. You can plant a seed of doubt into your subject, especially if a Strand has been formed. When re-configurating someone's subconscious, be advised that you must stay through the entire process. You can't be with your subject or subjects all the time, but you can plant Seeds....

SEEDS

Genesis 3:5 – For God knows that when you eat of it your eyes will be opened and you will be like God, knowing good and evil. The Holy Bible

Genesis 2:16-17 – And the Lord God commanded the man, saying "You may surely eat of every tree of the garden, but of the Tree of The Knowledge of good and evil you shall not eat. For in the day that you eat of it you shall surely die." The Holy Bible

Sura 20 (Ta Ha) Ayat 120 – "But Satan whispered evil to him saying "Adam shall I lead you to the Tree of Immorality and to the kingdom that never

declines?" The Holy Quran
Genesis 6:5-7 – "The Lord saw that the wickedness
of man was great in the Earth, and that every
intention of the thoughts of his heart was only evil
continually. And the Lord regretted that he had
made man on the Earth, and it grieved him to his
heart. So, the lord said, "I will blot out man whom I
have created from the face of the land, man and
animals and creeping things and birds of the
heavens, for I am sorry that I have made them."

The above verse proves God is not perfect.
Indicated from the usage of the word "Regret."
Regret comes only when the conscious mind admits
to the subconscious mind that it's made a mistake.
A self-admitted mistake is the realization of one's
own imperfection. Therefore, one can conclude that
God is not perfect, he's just powerful. That why
people don't love God, they fear God. You love the
perfect, you fear the powerful.

In my experience with Strands and
Receptors, Seeds were just as much apart of my
plans as the Strands themselves. Seeds, unlike
Strands, can have a good intention or evil intention.

A positive Seed example: Remember when
you were younger and in grade school? Remember
when you'd have guest speakers? They would have
a small amount of time to convey a large amount of
information. At the end of the lesson they would
plant a Seed intentionally. "My time is up but I will
leave you with this." Or they'd say" Here's one to
grow on." What was meant by "grow on?"

What grows? Seeds grow. But if the lesson
is over and the presenter is no longer there then how

does the lesson continue? This is the same question I had posed of Osiris some 25 years ago. At end of a lesson or Strand upon your exit you leave with a lead question. A precursor to the lesson to come. When you meet with your subject again, you'll find that they not only answered your lead question but are in the mid-way process into the next lesson or stage of the Strand.

If one wishes to build a Strand to be welcomed by many, then he/she must aim at the L.C.D. of the entire crowd. During a time of depression and despair, the man on the soapbox preaching about immediate employment and financial prosperity will have the majority of that crowds undivided attention. Since the conscious mind deals with the wants of man and the subconscious mind deals with the needs of man that Strand would be absorbed/uploaded directly to the subconscious mind. And since it's in the subconscious mind as a need, the entire mind will approve of any amount of money for this illusion of substance.

Example: Have you ever attended a religious service of some sort and the speaker seemed as if they were speaking to you directly? He could describe exactly how you felt, your position, and what you were willing to do about it. In the days of my parents, those men/women were known as 'Poverty Pimp.' They would rise to prosperity off of the pain of the people. This was no coincidence. It was by design.

I remember I was invited into the home of a young lady I was in the process of turning her out. I had a tight grip on her Receptors that I had conjured up and built from over the telephone. When I met her family, it was a household of single women. Man-hungry, attention starved, sex deprived, single women.

I could tell how they were introduced to me by the young lady I walked into the house with. One by one, she called out their names. And one by one, they strutted towards me as if they were models on the runway. The feverish way they shook my hand told me that they had been discussing me recently in a favorable light. Their eyes sung a song of affirmation. At the moment, I decided to flatten the Strand and expand it to encompass the entire family. There was a mother, an aunt and two sisters. One older sister and one younger sister. No father, uncles or brothers in sight.

I did the best I could to conceal my fangs. To conceal my identity or intentions until it was too late for them to change directions. I looked for my opening. I told my lady "Baby could you take my coat please?" I said it as I looked at her little sister. Her little sister smiled, but the older sister reached for my coat at the same time that my lady did.

My lady friend was attractive, but not as attractive as her younger sister. And not as voluptuous as the older sister. I saw for the first time my lady friend suffered from the "Jan Brady" syndrome. The middle child blues, the ignored one. I knew how I would play this out all the while keeping in mind "A bird in the hand."

When I was in the room, I never ignored the one I came with. My focus and attention never left my lady as her family's attention never left me. Thus, raising my lady's value within the household. This value could only be made possible in my presence. I could have planted a seed upon my departure, but it would have been a bit premature. By not planting a seed nothing will grow without my presence.

This plant of insidious design was still in its embryonic stage and required hands-on guidance. My lady's value had to be raised a little higher in order to drop Seeds. But the Strand was growing in size. The L.C.D. of the household was attention.

My next target was the matriarch, her mother. She was clearly in charge. Over the next couple of weeks, I gradually made my moves from family member to family member supplying a general feeling of euphoria throughout the family while systematically tending to each individual need as it arose. Thus, making myself everything to everyone without altering who I was.

At the time I was only 18 but the sinister nature of the IZM itself had me wrapped in my own Strand. I didn't have absolute control of my power at that age, although possessed it. I would end up ofttimes destroying my own Strand by tightening the grip too tight too soon. Also knowing when to let go is key to your success. Not letting go in time can cause you to suffocate alone with your subject.

I went through that family like a recessive gene. To this day I'm welcomed there. Webster's dictionary defines the word genius as follows; Genius – Great intellectual and creative power. 2 – A person having this power.

When I was growing up, the only genius I'd heard of was Albert Einstein and maybe Wile E. Coyote. What 'power' could the Webster's dictionary be speaking about? 'Creative power,' that's a peculiar way to describe an intellectual attribute. Webster's Dictionary's definition for Power:
1 – The ability to act effectively.
2 – Strength, might.
3 – The ability to exercise control, authority.

The word 'Ability' is mentioned two times in the definition of power. The word ability itself is defined as follows:
1 – The power to perform.
2 – A skill or talent.

In the definition of 'Power,' the word 'Ability' is mentioned twice. In the definition of 'Ability,' the word power is mentioned. What makes a genius so powerful? If you take the word Genius by the definition and take the word 'Power' by its definition and put them together it reads:
1 – Great intellectual ability to act effectively.
2 – Great intellectual strength and might.
3 – Great intellectual ability to exercise control, authority.
Very interesting I find this. Most people wouldn't equate genius with power. Webster seems to.
Words jump off the page. Buzz words; effectively, exercise control. Geniuses seem to be a little more

than bookworms according to Webster's Dictionary. What's make one a genius? Is it a high I.Q.? Is it an innovative idea?

What makes a genius is his/her ability to access areas of the brain inaccessible to mostly everyone. Thus, increasing the likelihood of groundbreaking achievements and cutting-edge discoveries that catapults mankind through lightyears of evolution. Without geniuses, the world would have no escape from the box in which to think outside of.

Why are most geniuses initially thought of as insane? Because the people who call them 'insane' have no basis in which to process what their senses are uploading. So, in order not to cause a delay in the processing process (shock), the conscious mind compartmentalizes the info in a section marked "Crazy."

Chapter 8
The IZM

The power we in This Life speak of is referred to as the IZM. Also known as the Darkside. Time dictates the agenda. There's a time to laugh, a time to cry. A time to be born and a time to die. A time to heal, a time to kill and so on and so forth. The IZM clarifies what time it is.

The universal element of time. Time ticks one way. The theology of time finds its function deeply rooted in the depths of mathematics. Math is the only exact science. The universal element of time manipulated and maneuvered only by its Darkside mathematics. Ergo, the phrase "Time is money," is an actual fact.

An example of the milestone manipulation of time through applied mathematics would be daylight savings time. An example of unapplied mathematical manipulation of time would be Leap Year. The separation of night and day as man's understands it is 24 hours. 24 time zones around the world. 4 in America 'Pacific, Mountain, Central and Eastern.

Homosapiens view day and night as flipped sides. Much like a coin having a heads (day) and a tails (night). The two sides opposite of one another. Man actually defines differences as such. Hence the phrase "They're as different as night and day". Giving credence to the once dogmatic view of the world being flat.

The truth is that life is not divided by two. The night merely means each has revolved to the dark side of the sun. Even the element of time has a Darkside. Mathematics being the root of all that is fact. It is the very breath of life in which all stems. True and living mathematics is universal itself for it is ever living, ever growing and infinitely expanding.

Numbers are birthed out of zero. The beginning of all which are counted is the number one. Then what number is the highest number? There isn't one. It exists not. Man has accepted the end of numbers as infinity. Infinity meaning never-ending. Ten digits, 0 – 9 much like our Solar System 0 being the sun and digits 1 – 9 being the 9 planets in which we chart time, distance, the future as well as the past.

Through the universal law of transference using mathematical science translated into a universal language inserted into man as well as all beings who inhabit Earth is called logic. Logic is not limited by borders nor language.

Through religion logically inserted into the brain via permission of the conscience mind and stored by the subconscious mind as fact. Through the windows; sight sound, smell, taste and touch theories enter the conscience mind. The information is reviewed by the conscious mind (processing center). Then the information is sent and stored in the subconscious mind as fact.

One of the best examples of this process is man's belief in God. Religion is man's way of making the question of creation and purpose of existence a fact. Thus, shutting down opposing or additional theories. God and or the theory of, can't exist nor make sense without the existence of evil and or the Devil.

A 360° degree view of knowledge, wisdom and understanding is necessary to become a master. The journey to this point is referred to as an "Eye Opening" (not eyes but referring to the third eye, the all-seeing, insight, foresight, sight beyond) experience. In religious terms it's referred to as an awakening. Some faiths even refer to it as being "Born Again."

Being born again is a logical impossibility if taken literally. An epiphany, an awakening, being born again or coming into the light out of the darkness. All saying the same thing. During an "Awakening," the third eye is opened in stages. These are called points of view or perspectives.

You have peripheral view, panoramic view, rear view, narrow view etc. Insight and foresight develop during the second stage of enlightenment. 360° degree eyes wide open is sight beyond sight. This can only be achieved after tasting the fruit grown from the Tree of Knowledge.

Earth has a Sun who's rays effect life on Earth. Its rays effect the growth of vegetation as

well as what we eat and when. The Moon effects
life on Earth also. As the sun effects the land the
mon effects the sea. The Earth is ¾ water which is
controlled by the lunar calendar. The human body is
also made up of ¾ water. The human body and
mind are affected by the lunar calendar. The dark
side of the Sun.

In order to understand anything to the point
where you've mastered it. One must embrace a
larger view. To learn anything inside out you must
be able to look at it from all angles. Then and only
then can it be properly manipulated to the point
where it becomes useful to its inhabited.

Example: Let's take a hammer. A hammer
can be a tool or a weapon depending who's hand
it's in and what purpose is the intent. A gun can
save lives. A gun can take lives. A cop and criminal
both wield the same mechanism with complete
opposite intent. Grave danger lies behind the hand
with power of no intent.

Democracy, a shared and desired concept by
many who enjoy its spoils and those who desire its
resources. One man, one vote, majority rules. In the
philosophy of power lies the intent of freedom. Out
of that intent flourishes it's dark side...capitalism.

Capitalism as history has proven has
motivated massive world wars, subjugation of entire
races into slavery and the Genocide of complete
populations worldwide. Capitalism was used to
justify such actions.

Communism's beautiful concept of all for
one and one for all. A financial system based on
group ownership created to break down dictators

and monarchies. A system where the majority poor share greatly in the spoils once totally owned and controlled by a select few. Communism's hard line approach to governing made evolution, compromise and growth virtually impossible. The man who refuses to grow, grows smaller.

Socialism coming out of the word "social" which means living in groups. Socialism having public ownership of good and services. Systems that were born to combat the complete control of man by the privileged few. The concept of unionizing entire populations with the intent of inclusion of all.

Political systems were created to give an alternative to religious rule. With Capitalism, comes an atheist state. With Socialism, the religious society becomes powerless in the political processes. Out of the light of Christianity also does the dark side of Christianity which is Imperialism.

Historically, one can't separate Christianity from the evil intentions of Imperialism. Out of the light of Islam also comes the dark side of Islam which is Terrorism. The two are forever intertwined to the point of coexistence. Fear and the power of it are absorbing the peace and strength that Islam delivers, much like a cancer or bacteria.

Allow me to expand on this fact of systems of power in depth. Because without proving my facts, my facts aren't fact at all, just opinion. I don't present my opinion. I let the irrefutable logical facts speak for themselves. I'm merely the messenger thereof.

Since the creation of man and the dawning of mankind, humans have been in search for truth, the balance of power and control, creation and evolution, religion and politics. Man seeks absolute power over his dominion. Man seeks to rule the world by ruling its inhabitants.

How can so many be controlled by so few? Why is it that a herd of over 100 gazelles run from only a few lions? The law of the jungle or system of the jungle that controls its inhabitants is "The Food Chain." Since humans widely do not practice or engage in cannibalism, man had to invent a parallel system of the food chain that man would most likely adopt.

Once man adopts a system into his subconscious, he then begins to implement this system into his conscious mind though practice. How to influence man enough to submit to the will of another man? You exploit and manipulate his thoughts and emotions by altering what is already there. What is already in man before anything has been uploaded by the conscious mind? The subconscious.

We as inhabitants of planet Earth are born with a certain amount of information in our brains (hard drive). Example: A baby is born knowing how to eat, cry, dance and laugh before it utters its first word. A baby of less than a year will move its head from side to side to show rejection (the word NO) without ever being taught.

The way man gets men to submit to the will of man is to tickle (stimulate) the senses it has been born with deep within the human psyche. You go to the source, the beginning. The first law of all living organisms is "Self-Preservation." If self-preservation is the first innate law of all that live, exist; Then with the usage of logic, one must deduce that the flipside or the dark side of such law is protection of that which threatens the termination of the first law.

The element that link the first law with its dark side is fear. The element of fear is used by parents to control children. Fear is used by the few, to control the many. Every current existing system of controlling human beings is based in fear. The flipside of a system of fear is the concept of reward and punishment.

The many fearful of the few is illogical. It's parallel to the 100-gazelle afraid of two lions. So, without a cannibalistic food chain how does man achieve this illogical equation? It achieves this by basing an adoptable system though fear.

Example: Religion- "Believe my doctrine and live forever on Earth divinely protected. Even after death you will live in the heavenly afterlife. Don't believe in my doctrine and suffer on Earth until death. Even after death you will suffer a fate worse than death eternally suffering in a place called Hell."

Out of a natural survival instinct that the homosapien is born with it will illogically upload and store incorrect, unprovable theories and store them as fact into the subconscious. Things stored by the subconscious via logic are never questioned once proven.

Example: $2 + 2 = 4$, there isn't anyone who can convince you that $2 + 2 = 5$. These logical facts are undeniable truths.

Man has adopted unprovable systems as a society as fact thus creating an eternal conflict. The brain is unable to solve for X, in other words, the brain can't locate the veritable. Thus, creating an external question/paradox.

The conscious mind creates an eternal conflict with the subconscious mind. This conflict is called "Doubt." Doubt enters when the war between the brain polar's (subcon and con) don't or can't agree. When the conscious mind overpowers the subconscious mind and forces it to store and process illogical information as logical fact with no truths to stand on is called "Faith."

Faith isn't belief in the unseen as most profess. Faith is belief in the unproven. Proof can only be achieved through the only perfect science. The science mathematics. If they believe a non-mathematical fact such as a fact about sports. It must be converted into a mathematically equation called logic.

Example: Shaquille O'Neal is tall. That's not a fact because the truth of that statement is in its perception which makes it opinionated. Why? Because if the question is posed to Yao Ming who stands 7'6" then he would see Shaquille as short. In order to store this fact, one could say, "Shaq is 7'1" and I'm 5'7" therefore Shaq is taller than I.

Numbers don't lie is a statement that implies numbers have a choice. Numbers can't lie is a factual statement. If one convinces many to adopt an illogical system and put this man-made illogical system into practice, the people who practice the system can and will be controlled by its author or

authors. That person will be kept in constant confusion and internal conflict. While perpetually in this dazed state of suspended animation, the authors can control the many as easy as a puppeteer controls its puppet's. Logic is based on one equation. A series of facts each proving the previous.
Example; If A + C = B and A + D = B then C equals D. If the first two statements are true then the third must be true. Logic is a direct road to the subconscious mind. Hypnosis is a technique I use through logic to bypass the conscious mind's objectivity. Hypnosis logically inserted can strengthen the subconscious enough to repair the conscious mind.

Things such as anxiety, P.T.S.D., shock, Bipolar, O.C.D., Addiction, schizophrenia etc. One can treat, and repair through a deep, self-induced, hypnotic state called 'meditation.' The flipside of fear-based control is the system of reward and punishment.

Example: Don't run a red light or you'll get a ticket. So, you stop at the red light even if no car is present. Why? To save lives or time? No, you stop to avoid a ticket. A man-made concept with words written on a thin piece of paper which has only the power over you than you give it. How? By adopting another man's notion of right and wrong via reward and punishment.

Power lies behind the ability to influence. Influence is the beginning of the control highway. Before one is influenced, they are impressed. Before one is impressed, they are interested. Before one is interested, they are introduced.

Before one is introduced, they are intrigued. What's intriguing about you? What do Capitalism, Communism, Socialism, Christianity, Judaism and Islam all have in common? They're all systems of power and control. Systems that have stood the test of time only threw the people who have adopted these systems as a way of life.

Once the human mind consciously inserts one of these "man-made" systems into itself, it logically rationalized it to be forever stored in its subconscious as fact. Once it becomes logical by way of mathematics, it becomes almost impossible to alter its significance to the human mind.

Example: Within the last century, we've seen many examples of this. America fought a war in North Vietnam and North Vietnam is still Communist. Hitler killed 6 million Jews during the Holocaust and those survivors were still Jewish. After W.W.II America and the Allied Forces defeated the Axis Powers. After the war, even in defeat, East Berlin remained Communist. The Berlin Wall couldn't be destroyed by war. It was only when Berlin decided to take the wall down did it come down. Thus, proving the absurdity of war or the use of force in order to change minds and or influence people.

The Darkside itself or one who studies the ancient art of mind control A.K.A. the Dark Arts. The common denominator that links all in all is called "The IZM." You will often hear pimps refer to their game as the IZM. The proper Shadow World term for a pimp is "A Gentleman of Leisure."

The proper Shadow World term for the power of pimps is the IZM. Using your thoughts, philosophy and actions to control the thoughts, philosophies and actions of all.

Groups such as the Illuminati (which means – the light or the enlightened ones), Freemasons, Skull and Bones, study and practice the mastery of the IZM. These groups or secret societies infiltrate mainstream society primarily throughout government and business which are the cradles of the world. Hence the saying "The hand that rocks the cradle is the hand that rules the world."

Government and business are the two main pillars holding up civilization. The support of civilization which includes the mandatory adopting of a system of religion or politics by the world's population being the only prevention of anarchy. Anarchy is step one or the beginning of the end of man thus the end of days. Therefore, justifying their main objective of world domination. Seeking affirmation and or justification only proves the acknowledgement of an existing superior.

This opens the door for the question; "Who do secular elitist serve as a superior?" If Satan is the Prince of Darkness, then who is the King of Darkness? Masters and their apprentices of the IZM practice and study its unlimited power. The acquiring of knowledge, wisdom and understanding of the depth of the mind, the Earth and the Universe's common thread.

The reading of the mind by studying the signs are as masterly as reading and studying a roadmap.

Once you know the roadmap, as you drive up and down the highway of life you will never be lost. The roadmap points to signs and signals along the highway. Identifying the signs lead to creating signs in order to manipulate your journey and the journey of man. The will of man.

What makes a man submit to the will of another man? Political and religious doctrines are man-made. Anything man-made is subject to fault. Man has accepted that last statement as fact yet will blindly follow a man-made political/religious doctrine. The eternal internal turmoil of man is the struggle to make the illogical, logical. Once anything becomes logical it is forever stored in the mind's subconscious, as fact.

Subconscious facts permanent as they are act as bricks that the conscience mind uses its architectural skills to build and construct stairs which lead to a higher level of consciousness; Knowledge, Wisdom and Understanding. The homosapian mind alone will never understand the total complexity of the IZM.

A key must be fashioned to unlock the mind. The key to the subconscious mind lies dormant in the hidden innermost resources of the conscious mind. Because man-made doctrines of religion and politics aren't logically inserted meaning acceptance by the subconscious mind leaving more questions than answers.

When solving a word problem, it has to be converted into a math problem in or to find the quotient. You can convert a fraction such as ¾ into a decimal .75 without changing the facts of the equation. The process of conversion is logic. Logic processes theory into fact. Logic transfers fact from the conscious mind to the subconscious mind. If a religious theory lacks logic, it will not ever be accepted into the subconscious. Once a religious or political philosophy makes logical sense (to the brain which is dissecting it) then it becomes irrefutable fact. This is what creates Radicalism and Fanaticism. There are they key elements for transformation(growth) of the human mind.

Once in an interview I explained my literary style. I explained that my books and instructional guides are not informational literature but transformational literature. What's the difference? When the brain reads instructional literature, it scans the document with its eyes, then the brain uploads it. The information is then processed by the conscious mind, whether or not the information makes it into the subconscious mind depends on its preconceived notion of fact.

Transformational literature is written in a mathematical code which makes it irrefutable. Transformational information bypasses preconceived notions by going straight to the logical part of the brain which controls what is stored by the subconscious. Logic acts as a protective filter for the subconscious. In order for the psyche to maintain balance, only logically based information make it into the subconscious.

When information defies logic and enters the subconscious it creates an imbalance. An imbalance between the conscious and subconscious causes insanity.

Insanity distorts the perception of reality. This makes deciphering logic an impossibility once illogical information gets absorbed as fact (brainwashing) by the subconscious. Logic is the only defense the subconscious has.

If by chance illogic gets uploaded into the subconscious and bypasses logic the result can cause a nervous breakdown. A nervous breakdown occurs when the conscious mind and the subconscious mind can't decipher the difference between logical and illogical. The conscious and the subconscious must work together. This is called "processing."

Imbalance creates insanity which directly effects processing. Information is uploaded into the minds (third eye/penial gland) via the five senses (hearing, sight, smell, touch and taste). Processing would be the equivalent of chewing then digesting food then deciding what gets used, what get stored and what turns into waste. When the mind can't process, it can no longer function, this is call shock. Shock can be as short as a few seconds or become a full-blown nervous breakdown which can last a day, a year or possibly permanent.

Example: A person can witness a murder and become frozen physically. They might not be able to move for minutes. The brain can have such difficulty processing information to the point where it renders the body frozen. This is called shock. Now look again: Capitalism, Communism, Socialism, Christianity, Hinduism, Buddhism, Islam, Judaism, Illuminati, Freemasons, Secret Societies, La Cosa Nostra, Satanism, Atheism etc.

Find the common thread. My master taught me that humans, animals, all living things only move for one of two reasons.
1) To obtain a gain
2) To avoid a loss.

1) The universal language is mathematics.
2) The universal law that all living species and elements faithfully follow without choice is self-preservation.
3). The universal language when spoken mathematics is converted to logic.
4) The universal religion that connects every financial, religious, secular, secret society, country, state, the planet as well as the Universe is called Hedonism.

Hedonism is the pursuit of self-pleasure. The pleasing of one's self even if that pleasure is derived from self-sacrifice. Hedonism is defined differently for different people. What brings you pleasure my not bring the next man/woman pleasure. But rest assured, every road leads to the same place called Hedonism.

Understanding the IZM is a 360° view of Knowledge, Wisdom and Understanding. The how's, when's and why's when it comes with obtaining the IZM. Come into the light but be forewarned that there is a Darkside. The IZM is alive for it is ever-living, always building and continuously growing.

Mickey Royal

Exit
by
Mickey Royal

*I once met a girl, who gave me her heart,
and I sold the Devil her soul.
Her heart taught me love, so I bought her
soul back, and the price that I paid was my
own...*

Other books available by Mickey Royal At Amazon.com, Mickeyroyal.com or wherever books are sold.

**The Pimp Game:
Instructional Guide.........................14.95
by Mickey Royal
The former Hollywood king reveals secret
techniques with proven results on mastering the
art of submission. A look inside the mind of the
master as well as a chilling peek into the shadow
world. A modern-day guide parallel to The
Prince by Machiavelli.**

**Along For The Ride....................14.95
by Mickey Royal
An autobiographical account of how Mickey
Royal establishes The Royal Family; an
organized stable of prostitutes, which runs with
the efficiency of a Fortune 500 company. At the
same time, this powerful family takes on crooked
cops, overzealous music executives, drug lords
and the Muslim Mafia to solve a six-year-old
murder mystery.**

**Uninhibited: A Cuckold Conspiracy
by Cheyanne Foxx.........14.95
Barry, an executive and husband finds himself
swept away in an erotic cuckold mystery. He
enlists the aid of close friends to unmask the
secret of his wife's innermost desires. Upon
doing so, he unleashes hidden treasures within
himself.**

**Other books available by Mickey Royal
At Amazon.com, Mickeyroyal.com or wherever books
are sold.**

**Pimping Ain't Easy:
But Somebody's Gotta Do It**...................**14.95**
by Mickey Royal
**Coffee, a journalism student on spring break
who has been given the assignment of a lifetime.
She follows Mickey Royal around for seven days
as she gathers intel for her mid-term. She soon
finds herself entangled in the shadow world and
embarks on an adventure she won't soon forget.**

**I'm Leaving you
for a White Woman**..............................**14.95**
by Mickey Royal
**Dennis, seeing no other way to solve the
problems in his relationship seeks the counseling
of a therapist. During his soul-searching
excavation, he un-earths repressed feelings of
emasculation and anxiety, due to decades of
systematic subliminally subconscious emotional
abuse at the hands of Black Women.
Painstakingly arriving to the conclusion that
many Black Men have. But until now, were
afraid to come forward.**

About the author

Mickey Royal resides in Los Angeles where he is currently writing his next book. Contact him on Facebook or at mickeyroyal.com   Email; mickeyroyal2016@yahoo.com

Mickey Royal resides in Los Angeles California where he is currently working on his next book. Mickey Royal is a pure novelist with years of experience as a playwright, columnist and erotic poet. He has been regarded as "Pure Genius" by the American Literary Society and "The premier writer of our time" by The Real Freeway Rick Ross. Mickey Royal himself remains an enigma. He has produced and directed over 100 adult films. With the success of his first book The Pimp Game: Instructional Guide, which has been shelved as a future classic alongside The Prince by Niccolò Machiavelli, The Art of War by Sun Tzu and The Prophet by Khalil Gibran. He's known in certain circles as a master teacher, an aristocrat of crime, a gangster, an all-around renaissance man, the most prolific writer today, a gentleman of leisure and true man of respect. His story is legendary. As a young gangster growing up in Los Angeles California, the work he put in has been verified and documented in many circles.

Mickey Royal is a former gangster, drug dealer, F.O.I., legendary pimp, paid enforcer (Italians, Russians, Mexicans below the border), pornographer and bestselling author. He possesses the unique ability to place the reader inside of the story by placing the story inside of the reader. Techniques exploited from his roots in Islam (His mother was a Black Panther and his father a child soldier from U.S.S.R via Mali) and Shamanism. His literature has been regarded as transformational. As an F.O.I. he trained under Martial Arts Master Steve Muhammad. As a youth he lived with Michael

Conception in Carson and was a staff writer for Grand Jury Entertainment. As a pimp he opened brothels, after hours, escort services, swing parties, adult bookstore, live voyeur shows and unionized prostitution, which led to pornography. As a pornographer he produced and directed over 100 adult films for Gentlemen's video, Heatwave, Cinderella films, Black Market, and Hustler amongst others (He produced and directed Pinky's only squirt movie called 'Pinky Squirts. In over a 20-year span has had thousands of women (prostitutes and pornstars). While at Wasco State Prison he was Keefe D's bodyguard at Wasco State Prison. The FBI (confirmed by FBI operatives and Las Vegas Police dept for the past 11 years) uses his book The Pimp Game: Instructional Guide as a textbook for agents to get into the minds and inner workings of Human Traffickers.

First arrested at age 5 for attempted murder in daycare. Arrested for Attempted Murder in early 20's in Tennessee. Attempted Murder in early 40's in LA. Arrested In Tijuana Mexico for Narcotics Trafficking. Mickey Royal was Married to former Pornstar Elizabeth Sweet aka Yogi. She was Raymond Washington's (Founder of the Crips Gang) former girlfriend. After his divorce, he was engaged to former Pornstar Cheyanne Foxx for 15 years. Mickey Royal is the younger brother of Jay Supreme (who produced 'This is how We Do It' by Montell Jordan and 'Back In The Day' by Ahmad amongst other hits).

Mickey Royal

The Pimp Game; Secrets of Mind Manipulation

Made in United States
Troutdale, OR
10/14/2023

13694909R00080